NICHOLSON

Visitors'
LONDON

Nicholson
An Imprint of HarperCollins*Publishers*

A Nicholson Guide

First published 1974
12th edition 1996

© Nicholson 1996

London maps
© Nicholson generated from the Bartholomew
London Digital Database

London Underground Map by
permission of London Regional Transport
LRT Registered User No 96/1496

Other maps © Nicholson

Nicholson
An Imprint of HarperCollins*Publishers*
77-85 Fulham Palace Road
Hammersmith
London W6 8JB

Great care has been taken throughout this book to be accurate,
but the publisher cannot accept responsibility for any errors which
appear, or their consequences.

Printed in Hong Kong

ISBN 0 7028 3150 6

74/12/1912

SYMBOLS AND ABBREVIATIONS

A   - Access/Mastercard/Eurocard
Ax - American Express
Dc - Diners Club
V   - Visa/Barclaycard

Average prices for a three-course meal for one
without wine but including VAT:
£   - £10.00 and under
££   - £10.00-£20.00
£££   - £20.00-£30.00
£££+ - £30.00 and over

(Reserve) - advisable to reserve
B - breakfast
L - lunch
D - dinner
◗ - open all day 11.00-23.00 Mon-Sat, 12.00-14.00 & 19.00-
        22.30 Sun (as a minimum; may be open all day)
(M) - membership required

Opening times
Many places are closed on Xmas Day, New Year's Day and Good
Friday, and general opening times are subject to change, so it is
always advisable to check in advance.

CONTENTS

ESSENTIALS ON ARRIVAL 4
Transport from airports. Hotel booking agents. Information centres. Transport in London: underground, Docklands Light Railway, buses, British Rail trains, taxis, minicabs. Telephone services. Money: exchange facilities, banks, tipping. Car and bicycle hire.

HISTORIC LONDON 14
Sights and buildings. Houses of the famous. Churches and cathedrals. Bridges. Statues and monuments. Commemorative plaques.

ANNUAL EVENTS 31
Daily ceremonies and annual events from January to December.

MUSEUMS AND GALLERIES 39
The major museums and galleries from the Bank of England Museum to the Wallace Collection.

OUT AND ABOUT 47
Parks and open spaces. Botanic gardens. Cemeteries. Walking tours. Coach tours. River trips and tours. Canal trips. Zoos, safari parks and fun days out. Stately homes. Day trips from London.

SHOPPING 60
Tax free shopping. Shopping areas. Department stores. Clothes stores. Antiques. Auctioneers. Books. Crafts. Food. Gifts. Markets. Shop-by-shop street maps. Size conversion chart for overseas visitors.

EATING AND DRINKING 77
A selection of London's restaurants by nationality (from African to Vietnamese) and by speciality (fish, vegetarian). Also where to have breakfast or afternoon tea; cafés and brasseries; London's best pubs (including riverside, music and theatre pubs); and wine bars.

ENTERTAINMENT 97
Theatre ticket agencies. Theatres. Open-air theatre. Opera, ballet and dance. Concert halls. Dinner and entertainment. Live music venues. Members-only clubs and casinos. Nightclubs and discotheques.

EMERGENCY INFORMATION AND SERVICES 107
Accident/ambulance. Babysitting and childcare. Car breakdown. Chemists (late-night). Credit cards. Hospitals. Late-night food. Late post. Lost property. Public lavatories. Wheelclamping.

MAPS 111
Street maps (each entry is map referenced to these 14 pages. For example, **7 B2** refers to map number 7, grid reference B2). Shopping map. West End theatres and cinemas map. Bus routes map.

ESSENTIALS ON ARRIVAL

Arriving in London can be daunting as there is so much to take in. However, with essential information at your fingertips, it doesn't have to be an unpleasant experience. Here is useful information you may need from the outset, which will allow you to enjoy all the delights London has to offer.

From airports to the city

Gatwick Airport

West Sussex. (01293) 535353. ***By train***: Gatwick Express (0171-928 5100) to Victoria Station (**7 B2**) Trains take *30 mins* and run from *06.20-20.50 (every 15 mins), 21.20-23.50 (every 30 mins), 01.00-06.20 (every hour on the hour) Mon-Sun*. ***By coach***: Flightline 777 (0181-668 7261) to Victoria Bus Station (**7 B2**). Coaches take about *1¼ hours* (longer in heavy traffic) and depart Gatwick at *05.20, 06.00; then every two hours until 22.00 Mon-Sun*. ***By car***: M23/A23 to central London, *approx 1 hour.*

Heathrow Airport

Bath Rd, Heathrow, Middx. 0181-759 4321. ***By tube***: (Piccadilly line) *approx 50 mins* to Piccadilly Circus (**4 E3**) and run from Heathrow *05.08-23.33 Mon-Sat, 06.40-22.46 Sun* and from Piccadilly Circus to Heathrow *05.46-00.21 Mon-Sat, 07.03-23.25 Sun*. ***By bus***: (0171-222 1234) A1 to Victoria Coach Station SW1 (**7 B2**) via Earl's Court, Gloucester Road, Knightsbridge and Hyde Park Corner. The bus takes about *1 hour* and runs from *06.30-20.00 (every 30 mins) Mon-Sun*. A2 to Woburn Pl WC1 (**1 G5**) via Holland Park, Notting Hill Gate, Queensway, Lancaster Gate and Paddington. The bus takes about *1¼-1½ hours* and runs from *06.00-22.00 (every 30 mins) Mon-Sun*. There is another bus service, Airbus (0181-897 3305), to Victoria Coach Station (**7 B2**) *06.40-20.00 (every 30 mins) Mon-Sun*. ***By car***: M4 to west London, *approx 30 mins,* but can take longer in heavy traffic.

London City Airport

King George V Dock, Silvertown E16. 0171-474 5555. Used by businessmen commuting to and from London for meetings. Flights go to Paris, Brussels, Rotterdam, Lille and Jersey.

By rail: British Rail from Silvertown to Stratford (Central line underground), then *30-min* journey to central London.
By bus: Shuttlebus service to Liverpool Street Station *every 20 mins Mon-Sun* (journey time *25 mins*). A shuttlebus service to Canary Wharf (journey time *12 mins*) allows passengers to connect with DLR to the City. No weekend service.
By car: The Limehouse Link to central London, approx *15 mins*.
Luton Airport
Luton, Beds. (01582) 405100. *By train*: to King's Cross Station (on the Thameslink line) (**1 G3**) trains take about *40 mins* and run from *05.00-08.00 (every 20 mins), 08.00-20.00 (every 15 mins), 20.00-23.30 (every 30 mins) Mon-Sun; at 00.35 (Mon-Sun) & 03.23 (Mon-Fri)*. Connecting buses take passengers to the train station, but there are no night buses between *22.50-04.55 Mon-Fri, 23.20-04.55 Sat, 23.50-06.50 Sun;* passengers must take a taxi at these times.
By coach: to Victoria Bus Station (**7 B2**) coaches take about *1¼ hours* and run from *05.30-22.00 (every hour, except 21.00) Mon-Sun (from 06.00 Sat & Sun)*.
Stansted Airport
Stansted, Essex. (01279) 622380. *By train*: to Liverpool Street Station (**2 G6**) from Stansted Station (underneath the airport terminal) trains take *41 mins* and run *every 30 mins* from *06.00-23.00 Mon-Fri, 07.00-23.00 Sat, 07.30-23.00 Sun*. *By coach*: to Victoria (**7 B2**) the coach takes *1½ hours* and runs from Stansted *06.40-18.55 (every 2 hours) Mon-Sun* and from Victoria *09.00-21.00 Mon-Sun*.

Hotel booking agents

Accommodation Service of the London Tourist Board   **7 B1**
London Tourist Board Information Centre, Victoria Station Forecourt SW1. Information and bookings. Personal callers only. *Open Easter-Oct 08.00-19.00 Mon-Sun; Nov-Easter 08.00-18.00 Mon-Sat & 09.00-16.00 Sun*. Also at Heathrow Airport (Terminals 1, 2 & 3). Personal callers only. *Open 06.00-23.00 Mon-Sun*. Charge. Accommodation advice line – 0839 123435. Credit card hotline: 0171-824 8844.
Hotel Booking Service   **4 D3**
4 New Burlington Place W1. 0171-437 5052. Knowledgeable service on hotels in London, Britain and worldwide. *Open 09.30-17.30 Mon-Fri*. Free.
Hotel Reservations Centre   **4 C6**
10 Buckingham Palace Rd SW1. 0171-828 2425. Also at Victoria Station, Platforms 7 & 8 (**7 B1**). 0171-828 1849. Bookings all over Britain. *Open 09.00-18.00 Mon-Fri*. Free.
Thomas Cook Travel Hotel Reservations   **7 B1**
All kinds of hotels in London, Britain and worldwide. Sales

desk at Victoria Station, opposite Platform 9. 0171-828 4646. *Open 07.00-23.00 Mon-Sun.* Also at the following stations: South Kensington, Earls Court, Euston, Charing Cross, King's Cross and Paddington. Also at Gatwick Airport. Charge.

Information centres

British Travel Centre   4 D3
12 Lower Regent St SW1. Personal callers only. British Tourist Authority Information Centre, incorporating a British Rail ticket office and a bureau de change. Book a room, a coach trip or theatre ticket, buy plane or train tickets or hire a car. *Open 09.00-18.30 Mon-Fri, 10.00-16.00 Sat & Sun (09.00-17.00 Sat in May-Sep only).*

City of London Information Centre   5 D2
St Paul's Churchyard EC4. 0171-606 3030. Information and advice with specific reference to the 'Square Mile'. Free leaflets and literature available. *Open May-Sep 09.30-17.00 Mon-Sun; Oct-Apr 09.30-17.00 Mon-Fri, 09.30-12.30 Sat.*

London Tourist Board Information Centre   7 B1
Victoria Station Forecourt SW1. Travel and tourist information for London and England. Most languages spoken. Hotel reservations, theatre and tour bookings, guide books and maps. Personal callers only. *Open Apr-Oct 08.00-19.00 Mon-Sun; Nov-Mar 08.00-19.00 Mon-Sat, 08.00-16.00 Sun.* The tourist board's Visitor Call service is updated daily and gives information on what to see and do in London – 0839 123456.

Other London Tourist Board Information Centres at:
Heathrow Central Underground Station
Heathrow Terminal 3
Liverpool Street Station   5 F1

London Transport Travel Information Centre   4 E6
55 Broadway SW1. 0171-222 1234. They will answer queries about buses and the underground. Free maps of the bus and underground routes, plus information leaflets in French, German and English are available. *Opening times of the information centre vary; phone for details. Telephone information service 24 hrs. Automatic telephone call queueing system.*

Other London Transport Travel Information Centres at the following underground stations:
Euston	1 F4
King's Cross	1 G3
Liverpool Street	5 F1
Oxford Circus	4 D2
Piccadilly Circus	4 E3
St James's Park	4 D5
Hammersmith (bus station)	

Heathrow Central
Victoria (British Rail station)   **7 B1**
Waterloo International Terminal   **5 A5**
Scottish Tourist Board   **4 E4**
19 Cockspur St SW1. 0171-930 8661. Tourist information on
mainland Scotland and the islands. *Open for leaflets and infor-*
mation May-Sep 09.00-18.00 Mon-Fri (to 18.30 Thur), 10.00-
17.00 Sat (Jun-Sep only); Oct-Apr 09.30-17.30 Mon-Fri (to
18.30 Thur). Open 09.30-17.00 Mon-Fri all year for bookings.
Wales Information Bureau   **4 D3**
12 Lower Regent St W1. 0171-409 0969. Leaflets and information for the visitor to Wales. *Open 09.00-18.30 Mon-Fri,*
10.00-16.00 Sat & Sun (09.00-17.30 Sat in Jun-Sep only).

On the move

London has a comprehensive system of public transport with
four different services – the bus, the underground (tube),
Docklands Light Railway (DLR) and British Rail overground
trains. It is one of the busiest in Europe, but if you take time to
work out your route carefully it can give an excellent dimen-
sion on London life.
See bus map on page 128 and underground map on the back
cover of this guide.
For information about buses and the underground call 0171-
222 1234; for DLR call 0171-918 4000.
For the latest update on the travel situation call **Travel Check**
(24 hrs) *on 0171-222 1200.*

THE UNDERGROUND
Commonly known as the 'tube', for the visitor to London this
is the simplest way of getting around. Very efficient in central
London and a good service to north London, although few
lines run south of the river, where British Rail offers a more
comprehensive service. The tubes run between *approx 05.30-*
00.15 Mon-Sat, 07.30-23.30 Sun. All tube stations have a
notice showing the times of first and last trains and timetables
are issued free at Travel Information Centres (see page 6).
Fares are graduated according to zones. Travelcards, giving
unlimited travel for one day, a week, a month or a year provide
considerable savings. Travelcards can be used on the underground, buses, DLR and Network SouthEast trains, and can be
bought at any tube station. Keep some 5p, 10p, 20p and £1
coins handy to use in the ticket machines. Cheap day returns
are available after *09.30 Mon-Fri* or *any time Sat & Sun.* Keep
your ticket to use in the exit machine at your destination.
London Transport enforce £10 on-the-spot fines if you are

found travelling without a valid ticket. **Smoking** is illegal anywhere on the underground, including in the ticket halls, on stairs, escalators and platforms, as well as in the trains.

DOCKLANDS LIGHT RAILWAY (DLR)

DLR is integrated with the underground and British Rail networks. It links Docklands with the City of London, Stratford and Greenwich, and extends to Beckton, serving the area between the Isle of Dogs and the Royal Docks. A direct shuttle bus to London City Airport is incorporated into the network. The red, white and blue trains are computer-operated, although they do have a guard/ticket collector on board. There are excellent views from their high viaduct route over the stretches of water which form the Docklands. Trains run between *05.30-00.30 Mon-Fri, 06.00-00.30 Sat and 07.30-23.30 Sun (Beckton branch does not run at weekends)*.

BUSES

Covering the whole of Greater London, the famous red, double-decker buses, with the open platform at the back, are the best way to see London, but they are slower than the tubes, especially in the rush hours *(between 08.00-09.30 & 16.30-18.00 Mon-Fri)*. They run from *approx 06.00-24.00 Mon-Sat, 07.30 23.30 Sun*. First and last times of bus routes are indicated on bus stops, but traffic can prevent buses from keeping to these times. Buses stop automatically at compulsory bus stops (white background with a red horizontal line through a red circle). At a request stop (red background with a white horizontal line through a white circle) you must raise or wave your arm to hail the bus, and if you want to get off at a request stop, you must ring the bell once, in good time. On driver-only buses, the bells are on the silver hand rails. On open platform buses, pull the cord overhead downstairs, and push the button at the top of the stairs upstairs. **Fares** are graduated according to zones. The open-platform buses have a conductor who will collect your fare once the bus is moving. The newer buses have only a driver who you must pay as you board the bus. Both give change but do not like being given notes. Keep your ticket until you get off.

Nightbuses run through central London from about *23.00-06.00*. All pass through Trafalgar Square. Consult *Buses for Night Owls* for timetables, available from London Transport Travel Information Centres (see page 6). Travelcards (except for one-day Travelcards) can be used on nightbuses.

BRITISH RAIL TRAINS

British Rail run InterCity trains all over Britain, and also Network SouthEast, which serves London and the suburbs. Most routes interchange with the underground – timetables are available from the British Travel Centre (see page 6) and from British Rail stations. These trains generally run *06.00-24.00 Mon-Sat, 07.00-22.30 Sun*. **Fares** are graduated and cheap day returns are available except during the rush hours *(08.00-09.30 & 16.30-18.00 Mon-Fri)*; you can also use Travelcards. The Thameslink service gets through London quickly, and goes from Luton Airport via West Hampstead and Blackfriars to Gatwick Airport, Brighton and Kent. Ask at any British Rail station for a timetable.The main British Rail terminals are:

Blackfriars   **5 C3**
Queen Victoria St EC4. Enquiries: 0171-928 5100. Trains to south and south-east London suburbs.

Cannon Street   **5 E3**
Cannon St EC4. Enquiries: 0171-928 5100. Trains to south-east London suburbs, Kent and East Sussex.

Charing Cross   **4 F4**
Strand WC2. Enquiries: 0171-928 5100. Trains to south-east London suburbs and Kent.

Euston   **1 F4**
Euston Rd NW1. Enquiries: 0171-387 7070. Trains to the Midlands, northern England and Scotland.

Fenchurch Street   **5 F3**
Railway Place, Fenchurch St EC3. Enquiries: 0171-928 5100. Trains to Essex.

King's Cross   **1 G3**
Euston Rd N1. Enquiries: 0171-278 2477. Trains to north-east London suburbs, the Midlands, northern England and Scotland.

Liverpool Street   **5 F1**
Liverpool St EC2. Enquiries: 0171-928 5100. Trains to east and north-east London suburbs, Cambridge and East Anglia.

London Bridge   **5 E4**
Borough High St SE1. Enquiries: 0171-928 5100. Trains to south-east London suburbs, Kent, Sussex and Surrey.

Marylebone   **1 B5**
Boston Place NW1. Enquiries: 0171-387 7070. Trains to west and north-west London suburbs and Buckinghamshire.

Moorgate   **5 E1**
Moorgate EC2. Enquiries: 0171-278 2477. Trains to north London suburbs and Hertfordshire.

Paddington   **3 E2**
Praed St W2. Enquiries: 0171-262 6767. Trains to west and south-west England and Wales.

St Pancras   **2 A4**
Euston Rd NW1. Enquiries: 0171-387 7070. Trains to the
Midlands, north-west England and north-west London suburbs.
Victoria   **7 B2**
Terminus Place, Victoria St SW1. Enquiries: 0171-928-5100.
Trains to south and south-east London suburbs.
Waterloo   **5 B5**
York Rd SE1. Enquiries: 0171-928 5100. Trains to south-west
London suburbs, west Surrey, and the south coast of England.
Waterloo International is the mainline terminus for channel
tunnel services.

GREEN LINE COACHES

These are express buses run by London Country. Most run
from central London to outlying areas within a 40-mile (64km)
radius. Main departure point is Eccleston Bridge SW1 (**7 B2**),
but there is another departure point on Regent Street just
north of Oxford Circus (**4 D2**). For information on schedules
and fares phone 0181-668 7261.

TAXIS

The famous London black taxi cabs, which can now also be red,
blue, green or even white can be hailed in the street. A taxi is
available for hire if the yellow 'taxi' sign above the windscreen is
lit. If the driver stops, s/he is obliged to take you wherever you
want to go, provided the destination is no more than 6 miles
(9.6km) – otherwise it is at their discretion. All taxis have meters
which the driver must use on all journeys within the
Metropolitan Police District (most of Greater London and to
Heathrow). For longer journeys the price should be negotiated
with the driver beforehand. There is a minimum payable charge
which is shown on the meter when you hire a cab. Expect to
pay extra for large amounts of luggage, journeys between
20.00-06.00, at weekends and on Bank hols. You can order a
black cab by telephone *24 hrs* a day, but this will be more
expensive than hailing one in the street as you will be charged
for being picked up as well as taken to your destination.
Computer-cab: 0171-286 0286.
Dial-a-Cab: 0171-253 5000.
Radio Taxicabs: 0171-272 0272.

MINICABS

These cannot be hailed in the street, and are indistinguishable
from private cars. Unlike black cabs, they are not licensed, nor
do their drivers take the same stringent test. The cars have no
meters, so it is essential to negotiate the price of each journey

in advance. They are usually cheaper than black cabs over long distances, especially *at night and weekends*. Look in the *Yellow Pages* for lists of minicab companies.

Telephone services

ESSENTIAL NUMBERS
999: Emergency (Ambulance, Police, Fire)
100: Operator
155: International operator
192: Directory enquiries
153: International directory enquiries
123: Speaking clock
Telegrams: dial 100 and ask for International Telegrams (must be a day in advance).

TO FIND A NUMBER
London residential directories are in two volumes covering the alphabet from A-Z. The business directory covers A-Z in one volume. In addition, *Yellow Pages* covers all businesses in London listed alphabetically by trade (volumes by region). For directory enquiries (for which there is a charge unless you are calling from a public telephone box) you should have the name and address of the person/company you wish to contact.

MAKING A CALL
Generally central London numbers are 0171- and Greater London are 0181-. If you are not sure which to dial, telephone the operator (100 – free) and they will tell you. It is not necessary to use the prefix when dialling within a zone. The *Code Book* lists all exchanges outside London (or the operator will tell you) including international numbers.

PUBLIC TELEPHONES
The old red telephone boxes have now almost entirely disappeared, to be replaced by glass constructions. They are usually to be found in groups around stations (tube and train), in hotels, pubs and public places. There are several types:
Coin-operated which take 5p, 10p, 20p, 50p and £1 coins (minimum charge 10p); coins must be inserted before you can dial, but if you do not get through the money will be refunded (it is best to use smaller denominations as percentages of larger ones will not be refunded).
Phonecard which accept only British Telecom phonecards, obtainable from newsagents, chemists, post offices etc, and in denominations from 20 units (£2.00) to 200 units (£20.00).
Mercury phonecard which accept only Mercury phonecards, obtainable from newsagents, chemists, post offices etc, or credit cards – A.Ax.Dc.V. (minimum charge 50p).

COSTS

These are assessed according to time of day, distance and length of call. There are two different rates: **Daytime:** *08.00-18.00 Mon-Fri* and **Cheap**: *18.00-08.00 Mon-Fri & all day and night Sat & Sun*. Cheap time for most international calls is *20.00-08.00 & all day and night Sat & Sun*.

Money

CURRENCY

The unit of currency in Britain is the pound sterling (£) divided into 100 pence (p). There are coins for 1p, 2p, 5p, 10p, 20p, 50p and £1, with notes for £5, £10, £20 and £50.

EXCHANGE FACILITIES

There is no exchange control in Britain, so you can carry any amount of money through customs, in or out of the country. The best rate of exchange is always to be found in a bank. Bureaux de change will exchange most currencies and will cash cheques, but charge more. They can be found at airports, main-line train stations, central tube stations and in the larger department stores.

American Express

6 Haymarket SW1. 0171-930 4411.	**4 E3**

Chequepoint Bureau de Change

13 Davies St W1. 0171-409 1122.	**4 C3**
222 Earl's Court Rd SW5. 0171 373 9515.	**6 B2**
Marble Arch, 540 Oxford St W1. 0171-723 2040.	**4 A2**

Eurochange Bureau

95 Buckingham Palace Rd SW1. 0171-834 3330.	**7 B1**
45 Charing Cross Rd WC2. 0171-439 2827.	**4 E3**
Paddington Tube Stn W2. 0171-250 0442.	**3 E2**
Tottenham Court Rd Tube Stn W1. 0171-734 0279.	**4 E2**

Thomas Cook

123 High Holborn WC1. 0171-831 4408.	**4 G1**
104 Kensington High St W8. 0171-376 2588.	**3 C5**
100 Victoria St SW1. 0171-828 8985.	**7 C1**
Selfridges, 400 Oxford St W1. 0171-629 9188.	**4 B2**
39 Tottenham Court Rd W1. 0171-636 2320.	**4 E1**

BANKS

Standard banking hours are *09.30-15.30 Mon-Fri* although many branches open *until 16.30 Mon-Fri and on Sat morning*. They are closed on *Bank holidays*.

TIPPING

Should be an expression of pleasure for service rendered and never a duty. It is possible not to tip at all if the circumstances justify this. These guidelines give some idea of the average tip:
Restaurants Many add on a service charge, usually 12½%, but do not always say so – if in doubt, ask them. They usually say if it is *not* included.

Taxis 10-15%
Commissionaires for getting a taxi. Up to £1 depending on the effort expended.
Pubs & bars Never at the bar, but buy the barman a drink if you wish. For waiter service in the lounge, from 20p per drink.
Hotels Almost all add it to your bill, usually 10%. Give extra to individuals for special service, from 50p.
Porters 50p-£1 per case depending on how far it is carried.

Car hire

*The law now states that **all** occupants of a car must wear safety belts. This includes the driver, and all passengers (although it only applies to back seat passengers if safety belts have already been fitted). **Don't** park on double yellow lines; it will result in a parking fine or wheelclamp (both are expensive).*
To hire a car you will normally need to be over 21 and to have held a licence, valid for use in the UK, for at least a year. Overseas visitors' licences are valid in Britain for a year. Prices differ greatly from company to company and depend on the make of car and the season. There is a basic daily, weekly or monthly charge and you will be required to leave a deposit.

Avis **4 B2**
8 Balderton St W1. 0171-917 6700. You can book a car for anywhere in London from here. *Open 07.00.20.00 Mon-Sun.* Worldwide reservations: 0181-848 8733.
Budget
0171-935 3518 or 0800 181181 for your nearest branch in London. *Open 07.30-19.30 Mon-Fri, 07.30-15.30 Sat & Sun.*
Hertz Rent-a-Car
Radnor House, 1272 London Rd SW16. 0181-679 1799. Branches throughout London, Britain and Europe. *Open 08.00-18.00 Mon-Fri, to 17.00 Sat.*

Bicycle hire

The bike offers an alternative and often more interesting form of transport. London has become far more geared to cyclists in recent years and there are now special cycle lanes on many roads. Danger to health from noxious fumes is not nearly as great as the benefit gained from the exercise of cycling. Explore streets, relax in parks and avoid parking difficulties!

Bikepark **4 F2**
Stukeley St WC2. 0171-430 0083. Mountain bikes for hire. Secure warehouse parking for 150 bicycles.
London Bicycle Tours **5 B4**
56 Upper Ground SE1. 0171-928 6838. Bicycle hire; also organises tours. *Open Easter-Oct. Phone for details.*
On Your Bike **5 F4**
52-54 Tooley St SE1. 0171-407 1309. Also at Lillywhites, 24-36 Regent St W1 (**4 E3**). 0171-915 4101.

HISTORIC LONDON

London's history begins in AD43, when invading Romans bridged the Thames. They built the London Wall around AD200, traces of which are still visible today. This was to determine the shape of what is still called the City of London for some 1300 years. Despite the devastation of three-fifths of the City during the Great Fire of 1666, no radical re-planning took place immediately within the 'Square Mile'. However, a massive scheme grew out of the ashes beyond the City which was to create the London we know today. Surrounding villages were absorbed and now give their names to central districts of the capital.

London's growth resulted from rising commercial importance (the City is still one of the world's major financial centres), the Industrial Revolution, and more recently, developing public transport which pushed new suburbs well out into the countryside.

London has, naturally, changed enormously through the years, but, despite the Blitz and decades of redevelopment, every stage of London's history can be traced through her buildings, monuments, churches and famous houses.

Historic sights and buildings

Admiralty Arch   **4 E4**
Entrance to the Mall SW1. Massive Edwardian triple arch by Sir Aston Webb 1910. A memorial to Queen Victoria.

Albert Memorial   **3 E5**
Kensington Gore SW7. Gothic memorial to Queen Victoria's consort, Prince Albert, by Sir George Gilbert Scott, 1872. *During restoration work, the memorial is covered. However, the adjacent Visitors' Centre houses an exhibition showing the extent and scope of the work.*

Apsley House   **4 B5**
149 Piccadilly, Hyde Park Corner W1. 0171-499 5676. Originally known as 'Number One London', home of the 1st Duke of Wellington. Robert Adam 1778, alterations by Wyatt 1828. Recently re-opened following three years of renovations.

BBC Broadcasting House   **1 D6**
Portland Place W1. 0171-580 4468. G. Val Myers 1928. Imposing headquarters of the British Broadcasting Corporation where the Director-General and Governors meet to discuss the BBC's broadcasting policy.

Bank of England   **5 E2**
Threadneedle St EC2. 0171-601 5545. The government and
bankers' bank and custodian of the nation's gold reserves.
Outer walls are the original design of Sir John Soane, architect
to the Bank 1788-1833. Interior redesigned by Sir Herbert
Baker 1925-39. Museum (see page 39) *open to the public*.

Banqueting House   **4 F4**
Whitehall SW1. 0171-930 4179. Inigo Jones 1619-25. Only
surviving part of Whitehall Palace, used for state and court
ceremonies. *Open 10.00-17.00 Mon-Sat.* Charge.

Barbican   **5 C1**
Silk St EC2. 0171-638 8891. Chamberlin, Powell and Bon
1955. Over 2000 apartments (some the highest in Europe
when built), a water garden, the restored St Giles Cripplegate
Church, a girls' school, pubs, shops, a museum and the
Barbican Centre (1982) – the largest arts centre in the country.
Open 10.00-20.00 Mon-Sun.

British Telecom Tower   **1 E6**
Maple St W1. 0171-580 6767. Eric Bedford 1966. Stands 580ft
(176.7m) high topped by a 39ft (11.9m) mast with radar aerial.
Houses telecommunications equipment and offices. *Closed to
the public*.

Buckingham Palace   **4 D5**
St James's Park SW1. 0171-930 4832. The official London
residence of the Queen. Built 1705, enlarged 1825 by Nash.
600 rooms, 12 occupied by Queen Elizabeth II and the Duke of
Edinburgh. The Royal Standard is flown when the Queen is in
residence. State Rooms *open Aug-Oct 09.30-17.30 Mon-Sun.*
Charge.

Burlington Arcade   **4 D3**
Piccadilly W1. 1819 Regency arcade famous for small, exclusive shops. Beadles still ensure obedience to rules forbidding
'singing, carrying large parcels, and running'!

Canary Wharf Tower
West India Docks, Isle of Dogs E14. Tallest building in the
United Kingdom, 800ft (244m) high, set in an 80-acre (35ha)
business and residential district with shops, offices, apartments, restaurants and waterfront promenades.

Carnaby Street   **4 D3**
W1. The first men's boutique opened in 1957. World famous
by the 1960s and the heart of fashion during the following
swinging decade, especially for pop stars. Still has a lively, if
not so fashionable, image.

The Cenotaph   **4 F5**
Whitehall SW1. Sir Edwin Lutyens (1920) to honour the dead
of the First World War, and now those who died in both World
Wars. The annual Service of Remembrance takes place here
in *November* (see page 38).

Chelsea Royal Hospital   6 F3
Royal Hospital Rd SW3. 0171-730 0161. Established 1682 by
Charles II for veteran soldiers. Fine, austere building, designed
by Wren and opened in 1689 admitting 476 army pensioners.
Stables 1814-17 by Sir John Soane. Fine carvings, several
royal portraits and a museum. *Open 10.00-12.00 & 14.00-
16.00 Mon-Sat, 14.00-16.00 Sun (closed Sun Oct-Mar).* Free.

Clarence House   4 D5
Stable Yard Gate SW1. Elegant stuccoed mansion by Nash
1825. Now home of the Queen Mother. *Closed to the public.*

Cleopatra's Needle   5 A3
Victoria Embankment SW1. Brought from Heliopolis, dates to
1500 BC. Presented by Egypt and erected here 1878.

Covent Garden   4 F3
WC2. Originally designed by Inigo Jones as a residential
square in the 1630s. Market buildings by Fowler 1830; Floral
Hall added 1860 by E.M. Barry, architect of the Royal Opera
House (1858). In 1974 the flower market moved to Nine Elms
(**7 D5**), but the area survived to become a flourishing new
community with an eclectic range of shops and places to eat
and drink.

Docklands
Stretching from Tower Pier to Beckton is London's Docklands.
The area has undergone massive change from a thriving,
commercial port through closure to regeneration. The London
Docklands Development Corporation (LDDC) was set up to
create a 'new city for the 21stC' incorporating riverside apartments, shops, restaurants and offices. Other areas worth
exploring are Butler's Wharf, and West India Docks.

Downing Street   4 F5
SW1. Built by Sir George Downing MP in 17thC. No.10 is the
official residence of the Prime Minister; No.11 that of the
Chancellor of the Exchequer; and No.12 is the Party Whips'
Office. *Wrought-iron gates prevent direct public access.*

Fleet Street   5 B2
EC4. London's 'Street of Ink', associated with printing since
Caxton, has now lost most of its newspapers as new technology
moved them elsewhere. Connections still remain.

Greenwich
Cutty Sark
King William Walk SE10. 0181-858 3445. One of the great tea
clippers, built 1869, now in dry dock. Explore the galley and
cabins. Next to it is *Gipsy Moth IV*, in which Sir Francis
Chichester sailed single-handed round the world in 1966. Both
*open Apr-Sep 10.00-17.30 Mon-Sat, 12.00-18.00 Sun; Cutty
Sark also open Oct-Mar 10.00-17.00 Mon-Sat, 12.00-17.00
Sun.* Charge.

Museum of Artillery
The Rotunda, Repository Rd, Woolwich Common SE18. 0181-854 2242. Pavilion by Nash, 1822. A renowned collection of guns and muskets, rifles, armour and early rockets from France, Burma, Britain and India. *Open 12.30-17.00 Mon-Fri, 13.00-17.00 Sat & Sun (to 16.00 Nov-Mar).* Voluntary donation.

Old Royal Observatory
Greenwich Park SE10. 0181-858 4422. Part of the National Maritime Museum. Founded by Charles II in 1675 and designed by Wren. Time and astronomical instruments; the Meridian Line; largest refracting telescope in the UK. *Open 10.00-17.00 Mon-Sun.* Charge (combined entry to National Maritime Museum and Queen's House (see page 43).

Royal Naval College
King William Walk SE10. 0181-858 2154. On the site of Greenwich Palace, Wren's beautiful baroque building, 1694, houses Sir James Thornhill's amazing Painted Hall (which took 20 years to complete). *Open 14.30-16.45 Mon-Sun.* Free.

Guildhall   5 D2
Off Gresham St EC2. 0171-606 3030. Built 1411-40 with alterations by George Dance 1789 and Sir Giles Gilbert Scott 1953. Great Hall used for ceremonial occasions – there was a banquet here to celebrate Queen Elizabeth II's coronation. Library established 1423. Medieval crypt the most extensive of its kind in London. Great Hall *open 10.00-17.00 Mon-Sat.* Free. Library *open 09.30-17.00 Mon-Sat.* Free. The Museum of the Clockmakers Company is contained within the library and is *open 09.30-16.45 Mon-Fri.* Free.

Hampton Court Palace
Hampton Court, East Molesey, Surrey. 0181-781 9500. Riverside Tudor palace built 1514 for Cardinal Wolsey and acquired by Henry VIII who greatly enlarged it. Later additions by Wren in the 1690s for William III and Mary. Sumptuous state rooms decorated by Vanbrugh, Verrio and Thornhill. Famous picture gallery of Italian masterpieces, the Orangery, the Great Vine and the Maze. Spectacular formal gardens. *Open Apr-Sep 09.30-18.00 Mon-Sun; Oct-Mar 10.15-18.00 Mon, 09.30-16.30 Tue-Sun.* Charge.

Houses of Parliament   4 F5
St Margaret St SW1. 0171-219 3000. Originally the Palace of Westminster and a principal royal palace until 1512: the roof of Westminster Hall dates from the late 14thC. Became known as 'parliament' or 'place to speak' in 1550. The present Victorian Gothic building was designed in 1847 by Sir Charles Barry and Augustus Pugin specifically to house Parliament and has over 1100 rooms, 100 staircases and over 2 miles (3.2 km) of passages. The Houses of Parliament and Big Ben – the bell

clock housed in the adjoining St Stephen's Tower – make up London's most famous landmark. *Admission to Prime Minister's Question Time by application to your MP (or embassy for foreign visitors). Admission to debates by queueing. OPEN 10.00-14.30 Wed, 09.30-15.00 Fri, from 14.30 onwards Mon, Tue & Thur. Tours of Westminster Hall and the Palace of Westminster by application to your MP.* Free.

Hyde Park Corner   4 B5

SW1. Constitution Arch and the Ionic Screen of three classical-style triumphal arches by Decimus Burton 1825. Once intended as an imposing and pleasing feature of the journey from Buckingham Palace to Hyde Park, it now swarms with traffic and underground pedestrians.

Inns of Court

Four great Inns of Court, dating from the 14thC, which act as a law school and have the exclusive privilege of calling candidates to the English Bar. Before they are eligible to be called, prospective barristers must pass the Bar exams, join one of the four Inns of Court and dine 24 times in the halls.

Gray's Inn   5 B1

Holborn WC1 (entrance from passage next to 22 High Holborn). 0171-405 8164. An Inn of Court since the 14thC, although the oldest surviving buildings are 17thC. Francis Bacon had chambers here from 1577 until his death. He reportedly laid out the gardens and planted the Catalpa trees.

Lincoln's Inn   5 A2

Chancery Lane WC2. 0171-405 1393. Lincoln's Inn is a private estate in the south west corner of Lincoln's Inn Fields. Entrances in Chancery Lane and Carey Street. Public admittance to view the buildings from *08.00-17.00*. The north lawn and chapel are *open 12.00-14.30 Mon-Fri. Admission to the chapel outside these hours and to the Hall and Library by application to the Treasury Office, Whitehall SW1.* Free.

Inner Temple   5 B2

Treasurer's Office, Inner Temple EC4. 0171-797 8250. The Inner Temple dates from 1505. Prince Henry's Room, above the Gateway (1610), is the oldest domestic building in London and home to the Samuel Pepys Club and Pepysian memorabilia. *Open 10.00-16.00 Mon-Fri by arrangement. Closed Sat, Sun, Bank hols & legal vacations.*

Middle Temple   5 B3

Middle Temple Lane EC4. 0171-353 4355. Dates from 1570. Together with the Inner Temple it comprises courtyards, alleys, gardens and warm brick buildings. *Open 10.00-12.00 & 15.00-16.00 (by arrangement) Mon-Fri. Closed Sat, Sun, Bank hols, Aug & during examinations.* Free.

Jewel Tower   **4 F6**
Old Palace Yard SW1. 0171-222 2219. 14thC surviving frag-
ment of the Palace of Westminster, once the safe for Edward
III's jewels, clothes and furs, now home to a collection of
objects found during excavations of the area. *Open Apr-Sep
10.00-18.00 Mon-Sun; Oct-Mar 10.00-16.00 Mon-Sun. Closed
13.00-14.00.* Charge.

Kensington Palace   **3 C4**
Kensington Gardens W8. 0171-937 9561. Bought by William III
and altered by the architects Christopher Wren and William
Kent. Orangery House by Hawksmoor and Vanbrugh for Queen
Anne in 1704. Queen Victoria was born here. Apartments still
used by members of the royal family. State apartments *open
09.00-17.00 Mon-Sat, 11.00-17.00 Sun (last admission 16.15).
Closed Bank hols.* Charge. *Closed for refurbishment at time of
publication. Due to re-open May 1996.*

Kenwood House (Iveagh Bequest)
Hampstead Lane NW3. 0181-348 1286. Robert Adam 1764-9.
Edward Guinness, 1st Earl of Iveagh's collection of paintings
including works by van Dyck, Reynolds, Rembrandt,
Gainsborough and Turner. Gardens and wooded estate of 200
acres (81ha). *Open Easter-Sep 10.00-18.00 Mon-Sun; Oct-
Easter 10.00-16.00 Mon-Sun.* Free.

Lambeth Palace   **7 F1**
Lambeth Palace Rd SE1. 0171-928 8282. Official London
residence of the Archbishop of Canterbury since 1197.
13thC crypt beneath the chapel and Tudor gatehouse.
Tours (restricted); application to the Booking Secretary.

Law Courts   **5 B2**
Strand WC2. 0171-936 6000. Massive Victorian-Gothic building housing the Royal Courts of Justice. More than 1000
rooms and 3½ miles of corridor. *Open to public 10.00-16.30
Mon-Fri. Over 16s only for criminal cases; over 14s for civil
cases.* Courts not in session *Aug & Sep but still open to the
public.* Free.

Lloyds of London   **5 F2**
Lime St EC3. 0171-327 6210. Impressive glass and aluminium
structure by the Richard Rogers Partnership (jointly responsible
for the Pompidou Centre in Paris). Spectacular at night, this
multi-faceted, 12-storey structure is the headquarters for the
international insurance market. Huge dealing room in a 246ft
(75m) high atrium housing the famous Lutine Bell. Viewing
gallery no longer open to the public.

London Wall   **5 D1**
EC2. Parts of the old Roman wall still survive at St Alphage
Garden, St Giles Churchyard, Cripplegate St EC1 (**5 D1**); Jewry

St EC3 (**5 G2**); off Trinity Square EC3 (**5 F3**); and in the Tower of London EC3 (**5 G3**).

Mansion House   5 E2
Walbrook EC4. 0171-626 2500. Official residence of the Lord Mayor of London, built 1739 by George Dance the Elder. Palladian mansion with majestic Ball Room, Banqueting Room and Egyptian Hall, lavishly decorated in 23-carat gold. *Open (to parties of 15-40 people) Tue-Thur by written application.* Free.

Marble Arch   3 G3
W1. John Nash 1827, based on the Arch of Constantine in Rome. Only senior members of the Royal Family and the King's Troop Royal Horse Artillery may pass through it. From the 14thC to 1783, this was the main spot for public hangings.

Monument   5 E3
Monument St EC3. 0171-626 2717. Wren 1671-7. Made of Portland stone, it commemorates the Great Fire of 1666 and stands at 202ft (61.5m), a foot in height for every foot in distance from where the fire started in Pudding Lane. Summit 311 steps up spiral staircase. Magnificent views. *Closed for renovation at time of publication; due to re-open April 1996.*

NatWest Tower   5 F2
Bishopsgate EC2. 1980. 600ft (183m) tower – tallest building in Britain until the Canary Wharf Tower was completed in 1990 (see page 15). Slender, shining structure with a curious pin-striped effect from the closeness of its vertical lines. Dominates City skyline.

Nelson's Column   4 E4
Trafalgar Sq WC2. By William Railton 1839-42, 145ft (44m) column surmounted by a 16ft (5m) stone statue of Admiral Lord Nelson by E.H. Baily, erected 1843. The statue is minus his eye and arm, both lost in battle.

Old Bailey   5 C2
Old Bailey EC4. 0171-248 3277. Central Criminal Court, on the site of the old Newgate Prison. The scene for many famous trials – Oscar Wilde in 1895, Dr Crippen in 1910, J.R. Christie in 1953 and Peter Sutcliffe, 'the Yorkshire Ripper', in 1981. Public viewing gallery. *Open 10.30-13.00 & 14.00-16.00 Mon-Fri. Minimum age 14 (must be accompanied by an adult if under 16). Photography not permitted.* Free.

Pall Mall   4 D4
SW1. Early 19thC opulence. Gentlemen's clubs were established on this street as exclusive havens for their members. Reform Club (No.104) by Charles Barry, from where the fictitious character Phileas Fogg began his trip *Around the World in 80 Days;* Travellers' Club (No.106) founded 1819; Athenaeum Club (No.107) founded for the intellectually elite.

Piccadilly Circus   **4 E3**

W1. The confluence of five major thoroughfares – Regent Street, Shaftesbury Avenue, Haymarket, Piccadilly and Lower Regent Street. Fountain and statue of Eros by Gilbert (1893). The world-famous neon advertising hoardings make it a far cry from its original elegant designs. The first, for Bovril and Schweppes at the turn of the century, caused a great scandal.

Regent Street   **4 D3**

John Nash, asked by George IV (then Prince of Wales) to construct a link from Carlton House (now demolished) to the royal country home near Regent's Park, not only designed the route for Regent Street but also most of the buildings along it. Initially acclaimed, its imminent destruction was celebrated in 1927 when George V and his Queen drove down its flower-decked length – it was then rebuilt from end to end.

Ritz Hotel   **4 D4**

Piccadilly W1. 0171-493 8181. Designed by César Ritz 1906. Archways based on the rue de Rivoli in Paris, interior in Louis XVI style.

Royal Albert Hall   **3 E5**

Kensington Gore SW7. 0171-589 8212. Originally built as the 'Hall of Arts & Sciences', prefixed with 'Royal Albert' at the last minute by Queen Victoria. Venue for a wide variety of events from organ recitals to boxing matches.

Royal Exchange   **5 E2**

cnr Threadneedle St & Cornhill EC3. Present building (the third) 1844 by Sir William Tite. Originally founded as a market for merchants and craftsmen in 1564, and destroyed in the Great Fire. The second building was also burnt down, in 1838.

St James's Palace   **4 D4**

Pall Mall SW1. Built by Henry VIII for Anne Boleyn and used as a royal palace for over 300 years. Still a royal residence; no members of the royal family live there at present. Foreign ambassadors and High Commissioners are still accredited to the Court of St James although actually received at Buckingham Palace. Courtyards only *open to the public.*

Savile Row   **4 D3**

W1. World-famous as the headquarters of the finest of London's tailors. Built 1730s as a residential street, it became fashionable amongst tailors from the mid-19thC.

Savoy Hotel   **4 G3**

Strand WC2. Richard D'Oyly Carte 1889. Impeccable and impressive standards. Monet painted Waterloo Bridge from its terraces. Still the favourite of the famous.

Soho   **4 D2**

An area bounded by Regent Street, Oxford Street, Shaftesbury

Avenue and Charing Cross Road. Only a handful of peep shows and strip joints remain from its seedier days. Now full of fascinating foreign food shops, restaurants, street markets and nightlife of all sorts. Chinatown radiates from Gerrard Street.

Somerset House   **4 G3**

Strand WC2. On the site of an unfinished Renaissance palace (1547-50) with a history of many royal inhabitants. Present building by Sir William Chambers 1776. Once housed the register of births, marriages and deaths in England and Wales (see Public Record Office on page 44); now holds the register of divorce, wills and probate, offices of the Inland Revenue and the Courtauld Institute Galleries (see page 40). *Public admittance to galleries only.* Free.

Spitalfields   **5 G1**

E1. This centre of silk-weaving in England was established by the influx of Flemish and French weavers in the 16thC and 17thC. The industry reached its height at the end of the 18thC and early 19thC when about 17,000 looms were in use and a large area of East London was dependent on these family concerns. Fournier Street has some good examples of Dutch-style houses of the time. The industry collapsed some 100 years ago, but the streets here are still steeped in history and tradition.

Thames Barrier

Unity Way, Eastmoor St SE18. 0181-854 1373. Steel fins form an impressive piece of modern engineering set up to stem dangerously high tides. Opened in 1984, it is the world's largest moveable flood barrier. The Visitor Centre houses an exhibition explaining the technology involved. Visitor Centre *open 10.00-17.00 Mon-Fri, 10.30-17.30 Sat & Sun.* Charge.

Tower of London   **5 G3**

Tower Hill EC3. 0171-709 0765. A keep, a prison and still a fortress, the Tower has served as a palace, place of execution and in its time has housed the Royal Mint, the Royal Observatory, the Royal Menagerie, and the Public Records. Now famous for the Bloody Tower, Traitors' Gate, the ravens, the Jewel House, the Armouries, Edward I's Medieval Palace and the Yeoman Warders. British monarchs imprisoned here include Edward III, Henry VII and Elizabeth I. Other prisoners have included Thomas More, Guy Fawkes, Sir Walter Raleigh, and Rudolf Hess, detained during World War II. Also the site of many executions including two of Henry VIII's wives – Anne Boleyn in 1536, and Catherine Howard in 1542, both of whom were given the privilege of a quiet execution on Tower Green. *Open Mar-Oct 09.00-18.00 Mon-Sat, 10.00-18.00 Sun; Nov-Feb 09.00-17.00 Mon-Sat, 10.00-17.00 Sun.* Charge.

Trafalgar Square   **4 F4**
WC2. Laid out by Sir Charles Barry 1829. Nelson's column
(see page 20) is surrounded by Landseer's four impressive
bronze lions, 1868. Fountains by Lutyens. Famous for political
rallies, pigeons and the excesses of New Year's Eve revellers.

Whitehall   **4 F4**
Wide thoroughfare once part of the ancient main route linking
Westminster and the City, now used for ceremonial and State
processions. Lined with Government offices including Old
Admiralty, Old Scotland Yard, the War Office, the Foreign
Office, Dover House, the Treasury, Horse Guards' Parade and
Banqueting House.

Whittington Stone
Highgate Hill N6. Near the junction with Dartmouth Park Hill.
The milestone marks the spot where tradition says Dick
Whittington, London's most famous Lord Mayor, heard the
Bow Bells chime 'Turn again, Whittington, thrice Lord Mayor
of London'.

Houses of the famous

Carlyle's House   **6 E4**
24 Cheyne Row SW3. 0171-352 7087. Modest Queen Anne
terrace where Carlyle lived for 42 years until his death in 1881.
Ruskin, Dickens and Kingsley were frequent visitors. *Open
11.00-17.00 (last admission 16.30) Wed-Sun & Bank hols
except Good Fri. Closed Nov-Mar.* Charge.

Dickens' House   **2 B5**
48 Doughty St WC1. 0171-405 2127. Regency terraced house
where Charles Dickens and his family lived from 1837-9. Here
he completed *The Pickwick Papers* and wrote *Oliver Twist* and
*Nicholas Nickleby. Open 10.00-17.00 (last admission 16.30).
Closed Sun & Bank hols.* Charge.

Freud Museum
20 Maresfield Gdns, Hampstead NW3. 0171-435 2002.
Exactly as it was when he died in 1939, the house in which
Sigmund Freud found refuge after fleeing Hitler in 1938.
Extraordinary collection of Egyptian, Greek, Roman and
Oriental antiquities and also the famous couch on which he
conducted his analyses. *Open 12.00-17.00 Wed-Sun.* Charge.

Hogarth's House
Hogarth Lane, Great West Rd, Chiswick W4. 0181-994 6757.
William Hogarth's country retreat from 1749 until his death in
1764. Relics and impressions of his engravings on display.
*Open Apr-Sep 11.00-18.00 Mon & Wed-Sat, 14.00-18.00 Sun;
Oct-Mar 11.00-16.00 Mon & Wed-Sat, 14.00-16.00 Sun. Closed
Tue, first two weeks of Sep & last three weeks of Dec.* Free.

Dr Johnson's House   **5 B2**

17 Gough Sq, Fleet St EC4. 0171-353 3745. 17thC house in the attic of which Dr Samuel Johnson compiled his famous dictionary. Lived here from 1748-59. Relics include his chair from the Old Cock Tavern and a first edition of his dictionary. *Open May-Sep 11.00-17.30 Mon-Sat; Oct-Apr 11.00-17.00 Mon-Sat. Closed Sun & Bank hols.* Small charge.

Keats' House

Wentworth Place, Keats Grove, Hampstead NW3. 0171-435 2062. The poet John Keats lived here from 1818-20, during which time his love affair with Fanny Brawne began. *Ode to a Nightingale* was composed in the garden in a single morning. *Open May-Oct 10.00-13.00 & 14.00-18.00 Mon-Fri, 10.00-13.00 & 14.00-17.00 Sat, 14.00-17.00 Sun; Nov-Apr 13.00-17.00 Mon-Fri, 10.00-13.00 & 14.00-17.00 Sat, 14.00-17.00 Sun.* Donations welcome.

Leighton House   **3 A6**

12 Holland Park Rd W14. 0171-602 3316. Eastern-style house, commissioned by Lord Frederick Leighton 1866. Arab Hall decorated with 14thC-16thC oriental tiles. Paintings by Leighton and Burne-Jones. Watts and De Morgan pottery. *Open 11.00-17.30 Mon-Sat. Closed Sun & Bank hols.* Free.

Wesley's House & Chapel   **2 D3**

49 City Rd EC1. 0171-253 2262. Methodist John Wesley's possessions and personal relics, and his tomb in the nearby chapel. In the crypt a museum tells the story of Methodism. *Open 10.00-16.00 Mon-Sat, 12.00-14.00 Sun.* Sunday service at *11.00*. Small charge.

Places of worship

In their buildings, ruins, sites and associations, London's churches and cathedrals represent nearly 1400 years of Christianity in Britain. The Great Fire of 1666 set the scene for Wren's rebuilding programme, including St Paul's Cathedral and 50 other churches. The 17thC and early 18thC saw many more churches built, to the designs of Nicholas Hawksmoor and Inigo Jones, and the Victorians produced a wealth of new churches in the 19thC.

Non-Christian religions also have their part in London's history, with synagogues as at Bevis Marks and the London Central Mosque in Regent's Park for London's growing Islamic community.

Entrance to all places of worship is free, unless otherwise stated.

All Souls, Langham Place   **4 C1**

Langham Place W1. 0171-580 3522. Nash's only church,

1822-4. Unusual style – Corinthian columns and needle spire. Interior refitted 1976. Exterior restored 1987-8.

Bevis Marks Synagogue 5 F2
Heneage Lane (off Bevis Marks) EC3. 0171-626 1274. Built in 1700, Britain's oldest surviving synagogue. Fine windows and brass chandeliers from Amsterdam.

Brompton Oratory 3 F6
Brompton Rd SW7. 0171-589 4811. Baroque style, Herbert Gribble 1834. The centre of Roman Catholicism until Westminster Cathedral was built 1903. Ornate interior and fine statues, some originals from Cathedral of Siena.

Chapel Royal of St John 5 G3
White Tower, Tower of London EC3. 0171-709 0765. The oldest Norman church in London, c1085. Original pillars still intact.

Chelsea Old Church 6 E4
Chelsea Embankment SW3. 0171-352 5627. Henry VIII and Jane Seymour married here in 1536. Original church dates from 1157, but the south chapel was rebuilt by Sir Thomas More. Severely bombed in 1941 and restored by Walter Godfrey. Many historic monuments.

London Central Mosque 1 A4
146 Park Rd, Regent's Park NW8. 0171-724 3363. Graceful building completed 1978, the religious centre for London's Muslims. A 75ft (25m) high golden dome and rich interior – marble floors, Turkish tiles. Reference library.

St Bartholomew-the-Great 5 C1
West Smithfield EC1. 0171-606 5171. Oldest church in London – the only surviving part of an Augustinian priory founded in 1123. Unusual oriel window and the only pre-Reformation font in the City. Many fine monuments.

St Clement Danes 4 F3
Strand WC2. 0171-242 8282. First built by Danes in 9thC, rebuilt by Wren 1681. Damaged during the Blitz, restored and rededicated in 1958 as the central church of the RAF. Bells ring 'Oranges and Lemons', made famous by the nursery rhyme of the same name.

St Giles Cripplegate 5 D1
Fore St EC2. 0171-606 3630. 12thC church rebuilt 1537 and restored by Godfrey Allen 1952 after bombing. Milton is buried here. Remains of the London Wall in churchyard.

St James Piccadilly 4 D3
Piccadilly W1. 0171-734 4511. Wren 1684. Restored by Sir Albert Richardson 1954 after serious bomb damage. Reredos, organ casing and font by Grinling Gibbons. Famous 'Father Smith' organ presented by Queen Mary 1691 and brought from Whitehall Palace.

St John Smith Square   **7 E1**
Smith Sq SW1. 0171-222 1061. Nicknamed 'Queen Anne's Footstool'. Built 1721-8 by Archer, gutted by fire 1742. Interior redesigned, then blitzed 1941. Restored to original design by a charitable trust. Opened as a concert hall 1969.

St Margaret's Church, Westminster Abbey   **4 F5**
Parliament Sq SW1. 0171-222 6382. Rebuilt 1486-1523 and many windows replaced after World War II. Splendid early 16thC east window and stained glass by Piper. Parish church of House of Commons since 1614. Samuel Pepys married here 1655, John Milton in 1656 and Winston Churchill in 1908. Caxton, Walter Raleigh and Admiral Blake are buried here.

St Martin-in-the-Fields   **4 F4**
Trafalgar Sq WC2. 0171-930 1862. Founded 12thC, rebuilt many times. Present construction by Gibbs 1722-6 with famous spire and portico. In 1924 the first broadcast service was conducted from here. Charles II christened here 1630; Nell Gwynne, Hogarth, Sir Joshua Reynolds buried here. Bookshop, art gallery, concert hall. Café in the Crypt.

St Mary-le-Bow   **5 D2**
Cheapside EC2. 0171-248 5139. Famous for its bells, used before World War II as time signal by BBC. True Cockneys are born within hearing distance of them. Rebuilt Wren 1670-83 and again by King 1956-62. Superb steeple – 217ft (66m).

St Paul's Cathedral   **5 D2**
Ludgate Hill EC4. 0171-248 4619/2705. Wren's masterpiece is the fifth cathedral on this site. The Whispering Gallery in the dome is particularly impressive – so named because the quietest whisper carries from one side to the other – 107ft (33m) away. Choir stalls and organ by Grinling Gibbons. Nelson and the Duke of Wellington are buried here; the Prince and Princess of Wales were married here in 1981. *Open 07.15-18.00 Mon-Sun except during special services.* Free. Crypt and Ambulatory *open 08.30-16.15 Mon-Sat;* Galleries *open 09.00-16.15 Mon-Sat.* Charge.

St Peter-upon-Cornhill   **5 E2**
Cornhill EC3. 0171-626 9483. Very fine church by Wren, 1677-87. Oldest church site in the City, reputedly AD179. Organ built by Schmidt. Fine carved screen.

Southwark Cathedral   **5 E4**
Borough High St SE1. 0171-407 2939. Originally founded in the 7thC, this is one of London's earliest Gothic churches. The tower dates to 1520 and the collection of monuments includes an oak effigy of a knight, dating to around 1275. The Chapter House has been redeveloped and now houses a restaurant. Cathedral *open 08.30-18.00 Mon-Fri.* Chapter House Restaurant *open 10.00-16.00 Mon-Fri.* Bookshop *open 10.00-16.00.*

Temple Church 5 B2
Inner Temple, Crown Office Row EC4. 0171-353 8559. One of only four remaining early Gothic round churches built by the Knight Templars, 12thC-13thC.

Westminster Abbey 4 F6
Broad Sanctuary SW1. 0171-222 5152. Original church founded by Edward the Confessor 1065. Rebuilding commenced 1245 by Henry III and largely completed by 1506. Towers completed by Hawksmoor 1734. Since William I it has been the coronation church of every new monarch and houses the coronation chair. Many royal and historic figures buried here, along with the Unknown Warrior, whose tomb represents the dead of World War I. Poets' Corner is the resting place of Dryden, Browning, Sheridan and Tennyson. Sculpted angels in south transept and fine tiled floors. *Open 09.20-16.00 Mon-Fri; 09.00-14.00 & 15.45-17.00 Sat. Closed Sun, services only.* Museum *open 10.30-16.00 Mon-Sun.* Nave and cloisters *open 08.00-18.00 Mon-Sun.* Small charge.

Westminster RC Cathedral 4 D6
Ashley Place SW1. 0171-834 7452. The headquarters of the Catholic Church in Britain. Completed 1903, with glorious marble mosaics. Widest nave in England with the early 15thC statue of Our Lady and Child. *Open 06.45-20.00 Mon-Sun (closes 19.00 in winter).*

London's bridges

Albert Bridge 6 E4
Three-span bridge 1871 by Ordish. Unusual rigid chain suspension. Tradition has it that soldiers crossing must break step because their marching rhythm may weaken the structure! Particularly beautiful at night when illuminated.

Chelsea Bridge 7 B4
Original bridge built 1858 by Page. Human bones and Roman and British weapons tell of an immense battle fought here. Entirely replaced in 1934 by a suspension bridge.

Lambeth Bridge 7 E2
The site of the first bridge at Lambeth was originally the only place where a coach and horses could cross the river. In 1633 Archbishop Laud sank the coach with his belongings whilst moving into Lambeth Palace! First bridge built 1861, replaced 1929.

London Bridge 5 E4
Reigned supreme as the only bridge for 500 years. Originally wooden construction built by Romans, replaced in 12thC with stone one carrying houses, shops and the heads of traitors on spikes. Replaced many times – in 1971 the granite construc-

tion by Rennie (1832) was shipped off in its entirety to Lake Havasu City, Arizona. Present bridge 1973.

Queen Elizabeth II Bridge
London's newest bridge, opened October 1991. The first bridge downstream since Tower Bridge built 1894. Designed to ease the weight of traffic through Dartford Tunnel. Largest of its type in Europe – twin towers 450ft (130m) high. Toll charges will be incurred until around the year 2005.

Tower Bridge   5 G4
Jones and Wolfe-Barry 1894. Designed to echo the Tower of London. It opens to allow tall ships to pass – each section of the double-bascule drawbridge weighs over 1000 tonnes but can be raised in under two minutes. High walkways afford excellent views of London and the Thames. Museum displays illustrate the workings of the bridge and a permanent exhibition brings to life the history, human endeavour and engineering achievement which created this famous landmark. *Open Apr-Oct 10.00-18.30 Mon-Sun; Nov-Mar 10.00-17.15 Mon Sun.* Charge.

Waterloo Bridge   4 G3
Rennie 1811. Opened on the anniversary of the Battle of Waterloo. Present bridge by Sir Giles Gilbert Scott 1937-42.

Westminster Bridge   4 F5
The watermen of the Thames were paid £25,000 in compensation when the bridge was begun in 1738. A stern warning went out when it opened – no dogs and the death penalty for anyone found defacing its walls! Present structure graceful cast iron, 1854-62 by Page.

Statues and monuments

Achilles   4 B4
Park Lane W1. 20ft (6.5m) bronze by Westmacott 1822. Caused an uproar as it was a nude statue dedicated by the 'women of England' to the Duke of Wellington.

Alfred the Great   5 D6
Trinity Church Sq SE1. Unknown origins, but undoubtedly the oldest statue in London, dating to the 14thC.

Boadicea   4 F5
Westminster Bridge SW1. Thornycroft, unveiled 1902. It shows the famous British queen riding with her daughters in a chariot.

Charles I   4 F4
Trafalgar Sq SW1. Hubert le Sueur, 1633. Ordered to be

destroyed in 1649, buried and kept safe until the Restoration in 1660. Royal Stuart Society lays a wreath here on the anniversary of his death, 30 January.

Sir Charles Chaplin   4 E3
Leicester Sq WC2. Doubleday, unveiled 1981 by the actor Sir Ralph Richardson. With his customary bowler hat and walking stick, he is appropriately surrounded by cinemas.

Sir Winston Churchill   4 F5
Parliament Sq SW1. 1973 by Ivor Roberts-Jones. Magnificent bronze statue of one of Britain's greatest statesmen, in naval overcoat, half-facing the House of Commons.

Oliver Cromwell   4 F6
Old Palace Yard SW1. Bronze by Thornycroft 1899. Holds a Bible in one hand and sword in the other. Paid for by Prime Minister Lord Rosebery as Parliament refused. Significantly, he stands with his back to the Houses of Parliament!

Elizabeth I   5 B2
St Dunstan-in-the-West, Fleet St EC4. Cast during the Queen's lifetime, 1586, by Kerwin. Originally stood over Lud Gate.

Eros   4 E3
Piccadilly Circus W1. Gilbert 1893. London's first aluminium statue, officially representing the Angel of Christian Charity. Paid for by public donations.

Sir Thomas More   5 B2
Carey St WC2. Stone figure by Smith 1866. More was 'the faithful servant both of God and the King. Martyred 5 July 1535'.

Peter Pan   3 E4
Kensington Gardens W2. Frampton 1912. Delightful figure of the fictional fairy character. Erected overnight as a surprise for the children. Carved animals at the base have been worn away by the strokes of tiny hands.

Captain Scott   4 E4
Waterloo Place SW1. Bronze by Lady Scott, erected 1915, of her husband in full arctic kit.

Victoria Memorial   4 D5
In front of Buckingham Palace SW1. By Brock, 1911. Impressive memorial to Queen Victoria which includes a fine, dignified figure of the Queen, the best of many statues of her.

Duke of Wellington   4 B5
Hyde Park Corner SW1. Huge bronze figure by J.E. Boehm (1888) of the Duke astride his favourite horse, Copenhagen. He looks towards Apsley House (now the Wellington Museum) where he lived.

Commemorative plaques

Since 1866, blue plaques have been used to mark houses and other buildings associated with famous people or events. There are now nearly 400 of them commemorating the lives of architects, artists, composers, politicians, scientists, soldiers and writers. The following are a selection:

Baden-Powell, Robert   3 D5
Founder of the Boy Scouts movement. Lived at 9 Hyde Park Gate SW7.

Berlioz, Hector   4 C1
Composer. Stayed at 58 Queen Anne St W1.

Bligh, William   7 G1
Captain of *HMS Bounty*. Lived at 100 Lambeth Rd SE1.

Browning, Elizabeth Barrett   4 A1
Poet and wife of poet Robert Browning. Lived at 99 Gloucester Place W1.

Brunel, Isambard Kingdom   6 D5
Civil engineer. Lived at 98 Cheyne Walk SW3.

Engels, Friedrich   1 B2
Political philosopher and novelist. Lived at 121 Regent's Park Rd NW1.

Gwynne, Nell   4 E4
Actress, mistress of Charles II. Lived at 79 Pall Mall SW1.

Handel, George Frideric   4 C3
Composer and musician. Lived and died at 25 Brook St W1.

Kipling, Rudyard   4 F4
Poet and story writer. Lived at 43 Villiers St WC2.

Marconi, Guglielmo Marchese   3 B2
Inventor and pioneer of wireless communication. Lived at 71 Hereford Rd W2.

Mozart, Wolfgang Amadeus   7 A2
Composer and musician. Composed his first symphony at 180 Ebury St SW1.

Pepys, Samuel   5 C2
Diarist. Born in a house on the site of Salisbury Court EC4.

Scott, Captain Robert Falcon   6 E4
Antarctic explorer. Lived at 56 Oakley St SW3, from where he left on his last fatal journey.

Shaw, George Bernard   2 E5
Dramatist and essayist. Lived at 29 Fitzroy Sq W1.

Turner, Joseph Mallord William   6 D4
Painter. Lived at 119 Cheyne Walk SW3.

Wilde, Oscar Fingall O'Flahertie   6 F4
Poet, dramatist and wit. Lived at 34 Tite St SW3.

Wren, Sir Christopher   5 D3
Architect. Lived at 49 Bankside SE1.

ANNUAL EVENTS

London plays host to a vast number of annual events, from colourful ceremonies to more obscure London customs such as the Doggett's Coat & Badge Race. For exact dates, times and places, where not given, contact one of the London Tourist Board Information Centres (see page 6).

Daily ceremonies

Contact the London Tourist Board Information Centre, Victoria Station Forecourt SW1, for further information.

Ceremony of the Keys   **5 G3**
HM Tower of London, Tower Hill EC3. 0171-709 0765. The Chief Warder of the Yeomen Warders, with an escort from the Brigade of Guards, locks the West Gates, the Middle Tower and Byward Tower. Listen out for the words spoken every night for 700 years – 'Halt! Who comes there?' 'The keys.' 'Whose keys?' 'Queen Elizabeth II's keys.' 'Pass the keys. All's well.' *21.40 Mon-Sun by written application, well in advance and enclosing a stamped addressed envelope, to the Governor, Queen's House, HM Tower of London EC3.* Free.

Changing the Guard   **4 D5**
Buckingham Palace SW1. Takes place inside the palace railings (in *summer* the crowds make it difficult to see much). The custom began in the days when the Life Guards were responsible for protecting the life of the monarch. An alternative is to see the Guards on their way from Wellington Barracks. They leave Wellington at *11.27.* The palace ceremony takes place at *11.30 every day in summer, alternate days in winter.*

Also at **Whitehall** (**4 F4**) at *11.00 Mon-Sat, 10.00 Sun,* leaving Hyde Park Barracks *10.28 Mon-Sat, 09.28 Sun;* and **Windsor Castle**, Windsor, Berks (01753) 868286 at *11.00 Mon-Sat in summer, alternate days in winter.*

Other daily events

Speakers' Corner   **4 A3**
Marble Arch corner of Hyde Park W2. A remaining vestige of the British tradition of free speech is this institution of impromptu discourses by unknown orators, usually on religion

or politics. Most lively on *Sun*. Also at Lincoln's Inn Fields
(**5 A2**) and Tower Hill (**5 G3**) *Mon-Fri lunchtime*. Free.

Feeding the pigeons   **4 F4**
Trafalgar Sq WC2. A famous tradition. You will soon find yourself accosted by touts who want to sell you bird-seed and
photographs of yourself. Beware, if you buy any seed, the
pigeons are likely to land on your head!

Annual events

JANUARY

International Boat Show   **6 A3**
Earl's Court Exhibition Centre, Warwick Rd SW5. 0171-385
1200. The latest pleasure crafts, yachts and equipment to
marvel at. Largest boat show in Europe. *Early Jan*. Charge.

January sales
Most stores have stock-clearing sales after the Christmas
shopping spree. Some fantastic bargains to be had, especially
at Harrods, but these go quickly and there are always huge
crowds, so get there early. The real fanatics camp outside
the stores, sometimes for days beforehand in a bid to be
first in.

Lord Mayor of Westminster's   **4 D4**
New Year's Day Parade
Information: 0181-566 8586. One of the largest parades in
Europe, with some 7000 performers. Marching bands, colourful
floats and veteran vehicles. Starts *12.30* at Piccadilly and ends
at Hyde Park (**4 A4**). *1 Jan*. Free.

Royal Epiphany Gifts   **4 D4**
Chapel Royal, St James's Place, Marlborough Rd SW1
Picturesque ceremony involving two 'Gentlemen Ushers'
offering gold, frankincense and myrrh on behalf of the Queen.
*Admission by ticket only; apply to the above address. 11.30,
6 Jan*. Free.

FEBRUARY

Chinese New Year Festival   **4 E3**
Chinatown, Gerrard St W1. Noisy, colourful affair in the
heart of the West End to celebrate Chinese New Year.
Papier-mâché dragons, extravagant costumes and brightly-lit
festivities animate the whole area. *Jan or Feb*. Free.

Great Spitalfields Pancake Race   **5 G1**
Old Spitalfields Market, Brushfield St E1. Teams of four in
fancy dress compete against each other in relays along a
section of old Spitalfields Market. Heats start *12.00*. To enter
call Alternative Arts 0171-375 0441. *End Feb or during Mar,
depending on when Easter falls*. Free.

MARCH
Chelsea Antiques Fair   6 E3
Chelsea Old Town Hall, King's Rd SW3. 0171-352 3619. Good selection of antiques and antiquities, with some real bargains. *Mid Mar and September.*
John Stow Memorial Service   5 F2
Church of St Andrew Undershaft, St Mary Axe EC3. The Lord Mayor attends this commemoration of London's first historian and places a new quill pen in the hand of Stow's statue. *11.30 Sun in Mar or Apr.* Free.
Oxford v Cambridge Boat Race
River Thames, Putney SW15 to Mortlake SW14. The annual rowing challenge between the dark and light blues (Oxford and Cambridge universities) has taken place since 1845. Plenty of vantage points from bridges, banks or riverside pubs – advisable to get there early for a good view. *Sat afternoon in Mar or Apr.* Free.

APRIL
Easter Show   6 F5
Battersea Park SW11. Colourful carnival; jugglers, stilt walkers and bands. Plus fairground, side stalls and various stage acts. *Easter Sun.* Charge (free for children under 14).
London Harness Horse Parade   1 C4
Regent's Park NW1. Fine breeds from Shires and Somersets to lighter-weight horses and ponies, carts, brewers' vans and drays are paraded around the Inner Circle at *12.00.* Judging starts at *09.30* and the public can inspect the horses before the parade. *Easter Mon.* Free.
London Marathon
Information: 0171-620 4117. The world's largest road race with competitors a mixture of international marathon runners, serious runners, joggers, celebrities and fancy dress 'fun' runners (usually raising money for charity). Good atmosphere with large crowds at both the start (Greenwich Park SE10) and finish (Westminster Bridge SW1 – **4 F5**). *Late Apr.* Free to spectators.
Tower of London Church Parade   5 G3
Tower of London, Tower Hill EC3. 0171-709 0765. The Yeomen Warders, in state dress, are inspected and parade before and after morning service at *11.00 Easter Sun.* Free.

MAY
Chelsea Flower Show   7 A3
Chelsea Royal Hospital, Royal Hospital Rd SW3. 0171-821 3000. Recorded information: 0171-828 1744. Superb floral displays burst into bloom in the grounds of the Royal Hospital. Exhibitions include extravagant landscaped gardens, fruit and vegetable displays, garden equipment and other

green-fingered accessories. *For four days, third week of May.* Charge.

FA Cup Final

Wembley Stadium, Wembley, Middx. 0181-900 1234. Climax of the English football season. *Some tickets from the above number, but the majority go to the two clubs whose teams are participating. Early May.* Charge.

Glyndebourne Festival Opera Season

Glyndebourne, nr Lewes, E. Sussex. (01273) 812321. Well-heeled Londoners don evening dress to hear superlative singing and dine out on the lawn, if the summer weather permits! Performances *May-Aug.* Charge.

Open Air Art Exhibitions

Artists display their work for the public to view (and hopefully buy!).

Victoria Embankment Gardens WC2 (**4 F4**) – *2-14 May & Mon-Sat during Aug.*

Royal Ave, King's Rd SW3 (**6 F3**) – *May-Oct 11.00-18.00 Sat.*

Works are also displayed against the railings on the Green Park side of Piccadilly (**4 C4**) and along Bayswater Road outside Kensington Gardens and Hyde Park (**3 D3**). *Sun morning all year round.* Free.

Rugby League Challenge Cup Final

Wembley Stadium, Wembley, Middx. Climax of the English Rugby League season, battled out in the mud at Wembley. *Contact the Rugby Football League (0113) 2623637 for details. Late Apr/early May.* Charge.

Rugby Union Cup Final

Twickenham Rugby Football Ground, Whitton Rd, Twickenham, Middx. *Phone 0181-892 8161 for details. Early May.* Charge.

JUNE

Beating the Retreat   **4 F4**

Horse Guards' Parade SW1. Colourful military display of marching and drilling bands acknowledging the 'retreat' or setting of the sun. Evening floodlit performances especially delightful. *For tickets phone 0171-222 7684. Early Jun.* Charge.

Derby Day

Epsom Racecourse, Epsom, Surrey. (01372) 726311. World-famous flat horserace. Also a fun fair and side shows. *1st week in Jun.* Charge.

Election of the Sheriffs of the City of London   **5 D2**

Guildhall EC2. 0171-606 3030. Lord Mayor and Aldermen of the City of London take part in a colourful ceremony. Tradition dictates that posies are carried to ward off 'the plague'. *Midsummer's Day, unless it falls on a Sat or Sun.* Free.

The Garter Ceremony
St George's Chapel, Windsor, Berks. Service dating from 14thC attended by the Queen. Preceded by procession with the Household Cavalry and Yeomen of the Guard. *Mon afternoon of Ascot week (usually 3rd week in Jun)*. Free.

Kenwood Lakeside Concerts
Kenwood House, Hampstead Lane NW3. 0171-973 3427. Bookings: 0171-413 1443. Classical concerts beside Kenwood Lake on Hampstead Heath performed by some of the most famous orchestras in the world. Often end with spectacular firework displays. *Sat evenings Jun-Sep*. Charge.

Lord's Test Match
Lord's Cricket Ground, St John's Wood Rd NW8. Recorded information on state of play: 0171-289 8011. Although confusing for the beginner, cricket is a British institution. The Test Match takes place here over *three or five days Jun or Jul*. Charge.

Royal Academy Summer Art Exhibition   **4 D3**
Royal Academy, Burlington House, Piccadilly W1. 0171-439 7438. Aspiring Cézannes and Hockneys enter their works to be admired and hopefully bought! Huge mixture of styles from oils to beautifully-crafted architectural designs. Be prepared for long queues. *Jun-mid Aug*. Charge.

Royal Ascot Races
Ascot Racecourse, Ascot, Berks. (01344) 22211. Famous event where hats and horses vie for attention. The Queen and other members of the royal party travel the course in open carriages each day before the race. *Three days – usually 3rd week in Jun*. Charge.

Trooping the Colour
Colourful pageant and procession to celebrate the Queen's official birthday. Royal party leaves Buckingham Palace (**4 D5**) at around *10.30* and proceeds along the Mall (**4 D5**) to Horse Guards' Parade (**4 F4**), then to Whitehall (**4 F4**) and back again. *Tickets awarded by ballot from The Brigade Major, Trooping the Colour, Household Division, Horse Guards' Parade SW1 (enclose a stamped addressed envelope). 11.00 Sat nearest 11 Jun*. Charge.

Wimbledon Lawn Tennis Championships
Church Rd SW19. Recorded information: 0181-946 2244. Height of the tennis circuit tournaments and one of the most famous championships in the world. Early evening is the best time to go to avoid the crowds. *Tickets for Centre Court, No.1 and No.2 Court are awarded by public ballot, but you can queue for tickets for the other courts on the day of play. Last week Jun & first week Jul*. Charge.

JULY
City of London Festival
Information: 0171-377 0540/248 4260. Arts festival held in the Barbican (**5 D1**), the Tower of London (**5 G3**), Mansion House (**5 E2**), St Paul's Cathedral (**5 D2**), many fine churches and the City's open spaces. Concerts, opera, exhibitions, poetry, drama, dance, jazz and many varied street events. *Three weeks in Jul.* Some events free, some charge.

Doggett's Coat & Badge Race
Information: 0171-626 3531. London Bridge (**5 E4**) to Chelsea Bridge (**7 B4**). Started 1715 to commemorate the accession of King George I. Sometimes called the 'Watermen's Derby', after the men who used to rule London's transport on the Thames, it is limited to six recently-qualified watermen. Colourful and fun event. *Late Jul.* Free.

Henley Royal Regatta
Henley-on-Thames, Oxon. (01491) 572153. Steeped in tradition, where smart outfits and even smarter picnics try to outdo each other on the riverbank whilst watching the skilled rowers do their stuff. *For exact dates phone the above number. Early Jul.* Charge (free for children under 14).

Proms (Henry Wood Promenade Concerts)   3 E5
Royal Albert Hall, Kensington Gore SW7. 0171-589 8212. Classical music festival culminating in the famous Last Night of the Proms at the Royal Albert Hall (see page 102). *Late Jul until Sep.* Charge.

Royal Tournament   6 A3
Earl's Court Exhibition Centre, Warwick Rd SW5. 0171-373 8141. Impressive military spectacle presented by the armed forces with much pageantry, military bands and daring feats. *Two weeks mid Jul.* Charge.

Swan Upping
Information: 0171-236 1863. Starts: Sunbury Lock. Ownership of the swans on the Thames is divided between the Dyers' Company, the Vintners' Company and the Sovereign. The Queen's Swan Keeper leads the keepers of the other companies and the swanherds to a fleet of boats, banners flying, for the trip up the reaches from London as far as Abingdon for the swan census. The cygnets are branded by nicking their beaks – one nick for the Dyers'; two for the Vintners'; the Sovereign's are left unmarked. *Phone in advance to find out exactly where the fleet is at any one time. Jul.* Free.

AUGUST
Notting Hill Carnival   3 A3
Ladbroke Grove and Notting Hill W11. Started originally as a celebration of West Indian culture, a lively, noisy, colourful

event with music, dancing in the streets and processions. *Sun* is children's day, and the main processions take place on *Bank hol Mon. Last Mon in Aug.* Free.

SEPTEMBER
Election of Lord Mayor of London   5 D2
Guildhall, off Gresham St EC2. 0171-606 3030. Colourful procession to celebrate the election of the new Lord Mayor of London. *Michaelmas Day.* Free.
Last Night of the Proms   3 E5
Royal Albert Hall, Kensington Gore SW7. 0171-589 8212. The culmination of the Proms concerts. Traditional rousing performance of *Land of Hope and Glory. Tickets by qualification system only – contact the above address. Mid Sep.* Charge.

OCTOBER
Her Majesty's Judges & Queen's Counsels   4 F6
Annual Breakfast
After a special service at Westminster Abbey, there is a procession to the House of Lords for the opening of the Law Term. *1 Oct.* Free.
Horse of the Year Show
Wembley Arena, Wembley, Middx. 0181-902 8833. Fine showjumping with many of the world-famous competitors under one roof. *Early Oct.* Charge.

NOVEMBER
Admission of the Lord Mayor Elect   5 D2
Guildhall EC2. 0171-606 3030. The Lord Mayor takes office. Colourful ceremony including the handing over of insignia by the former Lord Mayor. *Fri before Lord Mayor's Show. Mid Nov.* Free.
Christmas lights   4 D2
Oxford St and Regent St W1. Bright and imaginative illuminations line the streets and shop windows to celebrate the season. Ceremoniously switched on in *early Nov.* Free.
Guy Fawkes Night
Bonfires are lit all over London and Britain to commemorate the discovery of the Gunpowder Plot of 1605, by which Guy Fawkes and his fellow conspirators intended to blow up James I and Parliament. Organised public events are the safest and usually the most spectacular. *Evening 5 Nov.* Charge for organised displays.
London to Brighton Veteran Car Run   3 G4
Serpentine Rd, Hyde Park W2. Information: (01753) 681736. First held on 'Emancipation Day' in 1896 which celebrated the abolition of the Act stipulating that a car must be preceded by

a person walking with a red flag at 2 miles per hour. A colourful event with the contestants in period costume; only open to cars made before 1905. They start at *08.00* and aim to reach Brighton by *16.00*. *First Sun in Nov.* Free.

Lord Mayor's Procession & Show

The newly-elected Lord Mayor is driven in the 1756 State Coach, with a procession of about 140 floats, from the Guildhall (**5 D2**) to the Law Courts (**5 B2**) to be received and sworn in by the Lord Chief Justice. Biggest ceremonial event in the City. *11.10 second Sat in Nov.* Free.

Remembrance Sunday   4 F5

The Cenotaph, Whitehall SW1. Service attended by the Queen and the Prime Minister to honour the dead of both World Wars. Takes place at the eleventh hour of the eleventh day (or nearest Sun) of the eleventh month – the anniversary of the armistice of World War I. Poppies sold in the street to raise money for ex-servicemen. Get there early for a good view. *11.00 Sun nearest 11 Nov.* Free.

State Opening of Parliament

The Queen, in the Irish State Coach, is driven from Buckingham Palace (**4 D5**) to the House of Lords (**4 F5**) to open Parliament after the summer recess. Good views from the north side of The Mall – get there early. *10.30 1st week Nov.* Free.

DECEMBER

Carol services   4 F6

Westminster Abbey, Broad Sanctuary SW1. 0171-222 7110. Carol services on *26, 27 & 28 Dec.* Free.

Carol singing   4 F4

Trafalgar Sq WC2. Carols are recorded on tape so you can just listen or sing along! *All through Dec.* Free.

Christmas Tree   4 F4

Trafalgar Sq WC2. Each year the citizens of Oslo donate a Norwegian spruce (a custom dating from World War II). It is brightly lit from *16.00* and carols are sung around it. *Mid Dec-6 Jan (Twelfth Night).* Free.

New Year's Eve   4 F4

Trafalgar Sq WC2. Thousands gather in the square to bring in the New Year with massed singing of *Auld Lang Syne* and dancing round the fountains. Listen out for Big Ben tolling midnight. *31 Dec.* Free.

Tower of London Church Parade   5 G3

Tower of London, Tower Hill EC3. 0171-709 0765. The Yeomen Warders, in state dress, are inspected and parade before and after morning service. *11.00 Sun before Xmas.* Free.

MUSEUMS & GALLERIES

London's national museums and galleries contain some of the richest treasures in the world, collected during British explorations.They range from the vast British Museum to more recent and specialist additions and many now incorporate interactive displays and exhibits. Apart from the national art collections in the Tate Gallery, the National Gallery and the National Portrait Gallery, London is further enriched by other, once private, collections, now open to the public. It has long been a tradition that national museums and galleries are free, *but some have now found it necessary to introduce either* voluntary contributions *or a* fixed admission fee. *Special exhibitions usually incur an* entrance fee.

Bank of England Museum   **5 E2**
Bank of England, Bartholomew Lane EC2. 0171-601 5545. Charts the Bank's history from 1694 to the high-tech world of modern banking. Houses unique English banknotes, gold bars and the Bank's silver collection. *Open 10.00-17.00 Mon-Fri.* Free.

HMS Belfast   **5 F4**
Morgan's Lane, Tooley St SE1. 0171-407 6434. Cruiser built for the Royal Navy; now a museum showing its role during wartime. Film shows and lectures. *Open Apr-Oct 10.00-18.00 Mon-Sun; Nov-Mar 10.00-16.30 Mon-Sun.* Charge.

British Museum   **1 G6**
Great Russell St WC1. 0171-636 1555. The world's greatest collection of antiquities and the national collection of archaeology and ethnography with four million (or so!) objects ranging from prehistoric to modern. Pick up a copy of the free information map at the entrance to help you plan your way around. Highlights include the Rosetta Stone; Roman pavements; the Elgin marbles; 'Pete Marsh', the 2000-year-old murdered Lindow man found preserved in a Cheshire bog; and the Sutton Hoo treasures from the burial site of a 7thC Anglo-Saxon king. Also famous for mummies including those of humans, cats, crocodiles and even baboons. New collection of prehistoric art from Mexico. Exhibition on Sir Norman Foster's

Millennium rebuilding project. Domed Reading Room (1857) where Karl Marx studied and wrote *Das Kapital (open to members only)*. Next to the main hall is the **British Library** which contains, by law, one copy of every book, periodical or newspaper printed in Great Britain. Restaurant. Café. Excellent shop. *Guided tours (1½ hrs) at 10.30, 11.00, 13.30 & 14.00 Mon-Sat, 14.45, 15.15 & 15.45 Sun. Museum open 10.00-17.00 Mon-Sat, 14.30-18.00 Sun.* Free (charge for special exhibitions and guided tours).

Cabinet War Rooms   **4 E5**

Clive Steps, King Charles St SW1. 0171-930 6961. Intriguing underground suite of 19 rooms used by Winston Churchill and his War Cabinet from August 1939-September 1945 as a meeting, planning and information centre. See Winston's bedroom and the desk from which he made some of his famous war-time broadcasts. *Personal audio guide included in entrance fee. Open 10.00-17.15 Mon-Sun.* Charge.

Commonwealth Institute   **3 B6**

230 Kensington High St W8. 0171-603 4535. Near the grand gates of Holland Park, founded in 1887 to promote knowledge of Queen Victoria's Empire. Fun, friendly and lively, with lots of interactive and often humorous displays to show the history, people, landscapes, wildlife and crafts of the Commonwealth. Restaurant. Shop. *Open 10.00-17.00 Mon-Sat, 14.00-17.00 Sun.* Charge.

Courtauld Institute Galleries   **4 G3**

Somerset House, Strand WC2. 0171-873 2526. Notable assembly of paintings, furniture and drawings from six private collections. Fine examples of baroque furniture, Flemish and Italian Old Masters, the Mark Gambier-Parry Bequest and works by Manet, Renoir, Cézanne, van Gogh and Gauguin. *Open 10.00-18.00 Mon-Sat, 14.00-18.00 Sun.* Charge.

Design Museum   **5 G4**

Butler's Wharf, Shad Thames SE1. 0171 407 6261. Founded by Sir Terence Conran, shows examples of design past, present and future through a number of provocative exhibits. Furniture, gadgets and graphics. Blueprint Café renowned for good food. Bookshop, library. *Tours by prior arrangement. Open 11.30-18.00 Mon-Fri, 12.00-18.00 Sat & Sun.* Charge.

Dulwich Picture Gallery

College Rd, Dulwich SE21. 0181-693 5254. The first public art gallery in England (1814). Works by Claude, Cuyp, Rembrandt (including his portrait of Jacob II de Gheyn – stolen four times), Rubens, van Dyck, Gainsborough, Hogarth, Canaletto and Watteau. Shop. *Guided tour 15.00 Sat & Sun (included in entrance fee). Open 10.00-17.00 Tue-Fri, 11.00-17.00 Sat, 14.00-17.00 Sun. Closed Mon.* Charge.

Geffrye Museum
Kingsland Rd, Hackney E2. 0171-739 9893. Housed in several early 18thC almshouses, exhibitions of the British living room from Tudor times to the 1950s including the pre-fabs of the 1940s, a panelled Elizabethan Room, Regency Rooms, an early Georgian Room and a stylish 1930s room. Café. Shop. Gardens. Herb garden. *Open 10.00-17.00 Tue-Sat, 14.00-17.00 Sun.* Free.

Hayward Gallery   5 A4
South Bank Centre SE1. 0171-928 3144. Main venue for large-scale temporary exhibitions of both historical and contemporary art from America, Europe and Britain. Shop. *Open 10.00-18.00 Mon-Sun (to 20.00 Tue & Wed). Closed between exhibitions.* Charge.

Imperial War Museum   5 B6
Lambeth Rd SE1. 0171-416 5000. Popular museum concentrating on both the human and mechanical aspects of war. Vast collection of tanks, weapons and aircraft including a Mark I Spitfire. The Blitz Experience lets you see, feel and hear what it was like to be in London during the bombing of the 1940s. Operation Jericho is a flight simulator allowing you to experience flying with the RAF to release captured Resistance fighters. Good café. Shop. *Open 10.00-18.00 Mon-Sun.* Charge.

Institute of Contemporary Arts (ICA)   4 E4
The Mall SW1. 0171-930 0493. Three galleries with changing contemporary art exhibitions. Widely regarded as one of the most innovative art venues in the country. Also two cinemas, a theatre and video library. Restaurant. Late bar. Bookshop. *Open 12.00-01.00 Mon-Sun (galleries to 19.30, to 21.00 Fri).*

Jewish Museum   1 D2
129-131 Albert St, Parkway NW1. 0171-284 1997. Anglo-Jewish life, its history and traditions illustrated by ceremonial and ritual objects. *Open 10.00-16.00 Sun-Thur (last admission 30 mins before closing time). Closed Fri, Sat & Jewish hols.* Charge.

London Planetarium   1 C5
Marylebone Rd NW1. 0171-486 1121. Mind-boggling journey amongst the stars, space and cosmos! Thousands of projected images become clear with an expert guide to explain the astronomical mysteries. Shows about *every 40 mins Mon-Sun – phone to check.* Charge (combined entrance ticket with Madame Tussaud's available). No children under 5.

London Toy & Model Museum   3 D3
21/23 Craven Hill W2. 0171-706 8000. Vast collection of dolls, model cars, tin soldiers and countless other toys, spanning over 100 years. Also 90-year-old model coal mine and interactive airport control. Café. *Open 10.00-17.30 Mon-Sun.* Charge.

London Transport Museum   4 F3
The Piazza, Covent Garden WC2. 0171-379 6344. Tells the story of the world's largest urban passenger transport system and its effect on life in the capital since 1800. The displays include nearly 100 interactive and audio-visual exhibits. The Beck Gallery houses a permanent collection of maps and the Frank Pick Gallery features temporary art displays. Shop. *Open 10.00-18.00 (last admission 17.15) Mon-Sun.* Charge.

Madame Tussaud's   1 C5
Marylebone Rd NW1. 0171-935 6861. Amongst the waxwork effigies of the famous and notorious meet the Royal Family, Pavarotti, Nelson Mandela and Cher. Murderers lurk in the Chamber of Horrors. Celebrities mingle at 'The Garden Party'. Enjoy the sights and sounds of the seaside at 'The Promenade Pier Café'. Experience some of the greatest events that have shaped London's heritage at 'The Spirit of London', where visitors journey through 400 years of London's history in a replica of a black taxi cab. *Open 10.00-17.30 Mon-Fri (from 09.30 in summer), 09.30-17.30 Sat & Sun.* Charge.

Museum of London   5 D1
London Wall EC2. 0171-600 3699. London's biography from pre-history to present day with a variety of costumes and archaeological finds. The new Roman London gallery houses nearly 2000 original objects and the latest evidence from recent archaeological discoveries. Reconstructions include a Roman kitchen, the devastation of the Great Fire in 1666, a ghoulish cell from Newgate Prison, and Selfridges' 1920s art deco lifts. Restaurant. Shop. *Open 10.00-17.50 Tue-Sat, 12.00-17.50 Sun. Closed Mon except Bank hols.* Charge.

Museum of Mankind   4 D3
6 Burlington Gdns W1. 0171-437 2224. Ethnographic Department of the British Museum. Presents a series of changing exhibitions which illustrate the variety of non-western societies and cultures. *Open 10.00-17.00 Mon-Sat, 14.30-18.00 Sun.* Free.

Museum of the Moving Image (MOMI)   5 A4
South Bank SE1. 0171-401 2636. The story of moving images from Chinese shadow theatre to film, television and satellite. Actors in costume help you enjoy your visit and there are hands-on exhibits such as reading the news and animation. Restaurant. Bar. Shop. *Open 10.00-18.00 (last admission 17.00) Mon-Sun.* Charge.

National Gallery   4 E3
Trafalgar Sq WC2. 0171-839 3321. The nation's major collection of historical paintings, founded in 1824, covering European schools from the 13thC-20thC. A leaflet, available at the entrance, leads you to the 16 most famous paintings. Daily tours also highlight selected works. Famous painters include

Rembrandt, Rubens, Frans Hals, van Dyck, El Greco, Cézanne, Monet and van Gogh. The Sainsbury Wing, opened in 1990, houses a collection of early Renaissance paintings including works by Botticelli, Raphael and Titian with great attention paid to the display of the paintings as well as the works themselves. Restaurant. Café/bar. Shop. *Regular guided tours every day (contact the information desk for times). Open 10.00-18.00 Mon-Sat, 14.00-18.00 Sun.* Free.

National Maritime Museum
Romney Rd, Greenwich SE10. 0181-858 4422. In a beautiful riverside setting and incorporating the Old Royal Observatory and Queen's House, this is the world's largest collection of boats and navigational instruments. Ships' models, carved figureheads, weapons, pictures and fine silver collections tell the story of Britain and the sea, its navy, merchants and explorers. *Open 10.00-17.00 Mon-Sun.* Charge (combined entry to Old Royal Observatory and Queen's House).

National Portrait Gallery   4 E3
2 St Martin's Place WC2. 0171-306 0055. The former stipulation that for inclusion in the National Portrait Gallery you had to be dead has now been relaxed! Start on the fifth floor and work your way down for a comprehensive, chronological look at portraits of the famous and infamous from Richard II and William Shakespeare to Mick Jagger and Beatrix Potter. Special exhibitions on famous people in the arts, sciences, politics and armed forces; also sculptures, miniatures, drawings and caricatures. Bookshop. *Open 10.00-18.00 Mon-Sat, 12.00-18.00 Sun.* Free.

National Postal Museum   5 D2
King Edward Bldg, King Edward St EC1. 0171-239 5420. Thousands of stamps, stamp books and the Penny Black franked as the world's first stamp on May 6 1840. *Open 09.30-16.30 Mon-Fri.* Free.

Natural History Museum & Geological Museum   6 D1
Cromwell Rd SW7. 0171-938 9123. The Natural History Museum incorporates the Geological Museum, and displays a full range of exhibitions featuring the earth itself, known as the Earth Galleries of the Natural History Museum. Advanced and innovative methods of display involve, interest and entertain visitors of all ages. Among the most impressive sights is the massive skeleton of one of the largest land animals, Diplodocus, as well as the life-size model of a 90ft (27.5m) blue whale. The Dinosaur exhibition looks at every aspect of how dinosaurs lived and died, with large specimens and models. New garden sanctuary allows visitors to explore Britain's flora and fauna. Restaurant. Café. Shop. Both *open 10.00-17.50 Mon-Sat, 11.00-17.50 Sun.* Charge (free *16.30-18.00 Mon-Fri, 17.00-18.00 Sun & Bank hols*).

Public Record Office   5 B2
Chancery Lane WC2. 0181-876 3444. Public records from
the Norman invasion to the latest census, along with
treaties, writs and state papers. Star attraction is the
Domesday Book, a detailed survey of England in 1086. To
trace your roots go to St Catherine's House, 10 Kingsway
WC2 (0171-242 0262) where the register of births, marriages
and deaths is kept. *Open 10.00-17.00 Mon-Fri. Closed Sat,
Sun & B.hols* . Free.

Queen's Gallery   4 C5
Buckingham Palace, Buckingham Palace Rd SW1. 0171-930
4832. Contains exhibits selected from the Royal art collection,
regarded as one of the world's finest. Shop. *Open 09.30-16.30
Mon-Sun. CLOSED B.hols*. Charge.

Royal Academy of Arts   4 D3
Burlington House, Piccadilly W1. 0171-439 7438. Holds a
series of important special-loan exhibitions throughout the
year. Famous for its annual 'Summer Exhibition' which displays thousands of works by living artists for view and sale.
Can get very crowded at weekends. Café. Good shop. *Open
10.00-18.00 Mon-Sun*. Charge.

Royal Air Force Museum
Grahame Park Way, Hendon NW9. 0181-205 2266. The first
national museum covering all aspects of the RAF and its pre-
decessor, the RFC. There are 70 full size aircraft displayed in
hangars on a former wartime airfield. See the tiny Bleriot
monoplane, Sopwith Camel, Spitfire, Vulcan, Wellington,
Lancaster and Panavia Tornado, which saw extensive action
during the Gulf War. The history of flight is told through equipment, paintings and documents and you can try your hand at
piloting a low-flying Tornado in a simulator. The Battle of
Britain Hall has British, German and Italian aircraft including
Spitfires, Hurricanes and a Messerschmidt. Good restaurant.
Shop. *Open 10.00-18.00 Mon-Sun*. Charge.

Science Museum   6 D1
Exhibition Rd SW7. 0171-938 8000. One of the three great
national museums covering science, technology and medicine.
Includes many historic exhibits as well as more modern ones,
like the command module of Apollo 10. Ranging from a tiny
tea-making machine of 1904 to huge steam locomotives, the
exhibits show how modern scientific and industrial man has
emerged. Plenty of hands-on exhibits and interactive displays,
especially in the Flight Lab (third floor), and in the Launch Pad
(first floor). On the fourth and fifth floors is the Wellcome
Museum of the History of Medicine with exhibits covering
human history from the neolithic age to the 1980s. *Open
10.00-18.00 Mon-Sun*. Charge.

Shakespeare Globe Exhibition 5 D4
New Globe Walk, Bankside SE1. 0171-928 0202. Part of Sam Wanamaker's International Globe Centre, the central focus of which will be the rebuilt Globe Theatre (due to open in June 1996). The exhibition tells the story of Elizabethan theatre-going, the history of the Globe and the rebuilding project. A tour of the building site is included in the entrance fee. *Open 10.00-17.00 Mon-Sun.* Charge.

Sherlock Holmes Museum 1 B5
221b Baker St NW1. 0171-935 8866. Allegedly the house on which Conan Doyle modelled his imaginary 221b. The detective's domestic world has been recreated based on detailed study of the stories. *Open 10.00-18.00 Mon-Sun.* Charge.

Sir John Soane's Museum 5 A2
13 Lincoln's Inn Fields WC1. 0171-405 2107. Britain's smallest and most unusual national museum in the former home of Sir John Soane, one of England's most renowned and respected architects. Amongst the treasures are Hogarth's paintings the *Rake's Progress* and the *Election* series; antiquities, including the sarcophagus of Seti I (1370BC) found in the Valley of the Kings; and paintings by Turner, Watteau, Reynolds and Canaletto. New exhibition *Soane: Connoisseur and Collector. Guided tour 14.30 Sat. Phone for opening times.* Free.

Tate Gallery 7 E2
Millbank SW1. 0171-887 8000. Named after sugar millionaire, Sir Henry Tate, who donated his Victorian paintings as its foundation. It is both the museum of British art, with a collection from the 16thC to the present day, and holder of the national collection of international modern art. Works range from Impressionist to present day with often controversial new exhibits. The Clore Gallery holds the permanent Turner Bequest, including 300 paintings and 20,000 drawings by J.M.W. Turner. Due to the size of its collection, the Tate operates a policy of annual rotation, as they can only show a percentage of the works at any one time. Thus the star attractions mentioned below may or may not be on display when you visit – *phone the gallery in advance to avoid disappointment.* You may see Hogarth's self-portrait, Constable's *Flatford Mill*, William Blake's illustrations for Milton's *Paradise Lost*, or works by Monet, Seurat, Cézanne, Degas, Picasso, Matisse, Mondrian and British painters such as David Hockney, Ben Nicolson, and Augustus and Gwen John. Restaurant. Café. Excellent shop. Hi-tech "wand" offers 4-hour guided tours. *Open 10.00-17.50 Mon-Sat, 14.00-17.50 Sun.* Free (charge for special exhibitions).

Theatre Museum 4 F3
Russell St WC2. 0171-836 7891. A branch of the Victoria &

Albert Museum, right in the heart of 'theatreland' and the perfect place to discover the history of the English stage since the 17thC. Magnificent collection of playbills, programmes, prompt books, drawings, photos, models, costumes and props. Café. Shop. *Open 11.00-19.00 Tue-Sun.* Charge.

Tower Hill Pageant   5 G3
Tower Hill Terrace EC3. 0171-709 0081. London's first 'dark ride' museum tells the story of 2000 years of the City of London. Automated cars take you past life-like scenes depicting London's waterfront from early Roman settlements to the Blitz. Fascinating discoveries of recent archaeological waterfront excavations, dating from Roman, Saxon and medieval times, are also on display. Café. Shop. *Open Apr-Oct 09.30-17.30 Mon-Sun; Nov-Mar 09.30-16.30 Mon-Sun.* Charge.

Tower of London   5 G3
Tower Hill EC3. 0171-709 0765. The Tower of London has served as a palace, place of execution, has housed the Royal Mint and the Public Records and is now probably most famous for housing the crown jewels. Videos in the Jewel House show the 1953 Coronation and detailed television pictures of the crown jewels before visitors can examine them at closer range. The White Tower houses the Royal Armouries, and Edward I's Medieval Palace has been restored to recreate the atmosphere of the court in 1280. *Guided tours by Yeomen Warders every ½ hr, last tour 15.30 Mar-Oct, 14.30 Nov-Feb. Open Mar-Oct 09.00-18.00 Mon-Sat, 10.00-18.00 Sun; Nov-Feb 09.00-17.00 Mon-Sat, 10.00-17.00 Sun.* Charge.

Victoria & Albert Museum   6 D1
Cromwell Rd SW7. 0171-938 8500. National museum of art and design and the largest decorative arts museum in the world. An immense and wide-ranging collection; where else can you see a copy of Michaelangelo's 'David' and Naomi Campbell's shoes under one roof? Advisable to get the information leaflet at the bookshop to show you round the important exhibits. Restaurant. Shop. *Open 12.00-17.50 Mon, 10.00-17.50 Tue-Sun.* Donation welcome.

Wallace Collection   4 B2
Hertford House, Manchester Sq W1. 0171-935 0687. A private collection of outstanding works of art which was bequeathed to the nation by Lady Wallace in 1897. Splendid representation of the French 17thC and 18thC artists, including paintings by Fragonard, Watteau and Boucher. Home to the *Laughing Cavalier* by Frans Hals and also works by Rembrandt, Titian, Rubens, Canaletto and Guardi. Important collections of French furniture, Sèvres porcelain, majolica, Limoges enamel and armour. Shop. *Tours by prior arrangement. Open 10.00-17.00 Mon-Sat, 14.00-17.00 Sun.* Free.

OUT AND ABOUT

London is well-endowed with parks, gardens, commons, forests and heathland. There are over 80 parks within 7 miles of the centre of London – all that remain of early London's natural surrounding countryside. Left by accident, gift, or longsighted social intention, they provide a welcome breathing space. The royal parks are still the property of the Crown and were originally the grounds of royal homes or palaces. All parks are free to enter, but there may be charges to use the facilities within them.

Parks and open spaces

Alexandra Park
N22. 0181-365 2121. 196 acres (78ha) including Alexandra Palace, burnt to the ground six days after it was built in 1873. Rebuilt in 1936, it was again severely damaged by fire in 1980 and is now a multi-purpose entertainments and exhibition centre. Excellent views of the London skyline. Café. Park *open 24 hrs Mon-Sun*. **Facilities**: animal enclosure, parkland walk, boating lake, children's playground, conservation area, pitch and putt, playing fields, ski slope, ice rink.

Battersea Park   6 F5
SW11. 0181-871 7530. 200-acre (81ha) park opened 1853 by Queen Victoria. Festival Pleasure Gardens laid out in 1951 to celebrate the Festival of Britain. London Peace Pagoda built 1985 by monks and nuns of the Japanese Buddhist order Nipponzan Myohoji. Based on ancient Indian and Japanese designs, it stands at 110ft (33.5m) and has a double roof. Park *open dawn-dusk*. Playing fields, athletics track, tennis courts *open 08.00-dusk*. **Facilities**: all-weather sports surface, athletics track, boating and fishing lake, botanical garden (greenhouse *open 09.30-dusk*), bowling green, children's zoo, deer park, floodlit football pitch, playing fields, tennis, café, art gallery.

Blackheath
SE3. 0181-854 8888. 275 acres (111.4ha) of open grassland – a prime site for kite-flying and watching the sunset. Good views from all directions, especially Point Hill. The scene for many sporting events. Occasional festivals and fairs at *Easter, spring and late summer Bank hols*. Park *open 24 hrs Mon-Sun*. **Facilities**: bowling, cricket, model boat sailing, soccer, tennis.

Crystal Palace Park

SE20. 0181-778 7148. 200 acres (80ha) of park named after Paxton's 1851 Great Exhibition building, moved here from Hyde Park but burnt down in 1936; the vast, impressive ruins still remain. National Youth & Sports Centre opened 1964 with a stadium for 12,000 spectators. In amongst the boating lakes are 20 life-sized replicas of large prehistoric animals. Park *open 07.30-½ hr before dusk Mon-Sun*. **Facilities**: boating and pedalos, children's farm, circular maze, dry ski slope, fishing, mini fair, mini steam train, ranger guided walks, shire horse cart rides, sports centre.

Green Park   4 C5

SW1. 0171-930 1793. No statues or lakes – just 53 acres (22ha) of grass and an abundance of lime, plane and hawthorn trees. Ideal for picnics; a favourite spot for office workers at *lunchtime in summer. Open dawn-dusk Mon-Sun.*

Greenwich Park

SE10. 0181-858 2608. A royal park, gaining its royal connections with Henry VIII whose favourite residence was Greenwich Palace (the Royal Naval College now occupies the site). Excellent panoramic views. 200 acres (81ha) with avenues sloping down to the Thames, lined with chestnut trees and 13 acres (5.3ha) of wooded deer park. The National Maritime Museum and the Old Royal Observatory are within the park and the London Marathon starts from here in *spring*. Bandstand used in *summer. Park open Apr-Oct 05.00 (for pedestrians – 07.00 for traffic)-22.00 Mon-Sun; Nov-Mar 07.00-18.00 (or dusk) Mon-Sun*. **Facilities**: boating pool, children's playground, cricket, rugby, tennis.

Hampstead Heath

(including Kenwood, Golders Hill Park, Parliament Hill) NW3. 0171-485 4491. Open and hilly with a feel of real countryside; 800 acres (324ha) of park and woods with fine views of London. Crowded on *Bank hols* with visitors to the famous fair and equally famous pubs, the Bull & Bush, Spaniard's Inn and Jack Straw's Castle. Open-air concerts at Kenwood in *summer*. Parliament Hill, 320ft (110m), is a good spot for kite-flying and excellent views. Heath *open 24 hrs Mon-Sun*. Kenwood and Golders Hill *open dawn-dusk*. **Facilities**: adventure playground, athletics track, boating and fishing lakes, children's zoo, cricket, football, horse-riding (permit holders only), open-air swimming in several ponds, rounders, rugby, tennis.

Hampton Court & Bushy Park

Surrey. 0181-781 9500. 2000 acres (810ha) of royal park, the formal gardens of the great Tudor palace, Hampton Court, with ancient courtyards, superb flower gardens, the famous

Maze, the Great Vine planted in 1768 and the recently restored Privy Garden. **Bushy Park** is natural parkland with an artificial plantation, aquatic plants and ponds. Two herds of deer, fallow and red, roam throughout. Both parks have many fine avenues including the mile-long Chestnut Avenue in Bushy Park. Both parks *open 07.00-dusk Mon-Sun.*

Holland Park   3 A5
W8. 0171-602 2226. Behind the bustle of Kensington High Street are 55 acres (22.3ha) of calm and secluded lawns and gardens with peacocks, peafowl and pheasants. Once the private garden of Holland House, the Dutch garden dates from 1812 with fine bedding displays, iris and rose gardens, a yucca lawn, Japanese garden and the Orangery. Also a remarkable woodland of 28 acres (11.3ha) containing 3000 species of rare British trees and plants. Open-air theatre in *summer.* Café. Park *open summer 07.30-sunset Mon-Sun; winter 07.30-dusk Mon-Sun.* Restaurant looks out onto Flower Garden which is illuminated at night. **Facilities**: adventure playground, cricket, football, putting green, squash, tennis.

Hyde Park   3 F4
W1. 0171-298 2100. A royal park since 1536, once part of the forest used by Henry VIII for hunting wild boar and bulls. 360 acres (137.7ha) of parkland, walks, Rotten Row for horse-riders, and the Serpentine – a fine lake, created originally from six ponds, now used for boating and swimming. Serpentine Bridge by George Rennie, 1826. Speakers' Corner, where anyone can speak about anything, is near Marble Arch – public executions were held at the Tyburn gallows, where Marble Arch now stands, until 1783. Bandstand used in *summer.* Park *open 05.00-24.00 Mon-Sun.* The Lido *open May-Sep 10.00-18.00 Mon-Sun.* Charge for swimming. **Facilities**: boating lake, children's playground, open-air swimming, tennis.

Kensington Gardens   3 D4
W8. 0171-724 3104. A formal and elegant addition to Hyde Park. 75 acres (111.4ha) of royal park, containing William III's Kensington Palace, Queen Anne's Orangery, the peaceful 'Sunken Garden', and the Round Pond, perfect for sailing model boats. The Broad Walk, originally flanked by ancient elms, is now replanted with fragrant limes and maples, and the nearby 'Flower Walk' is home to birds such as woodpeckers, flycatchers and tree-creepers. Queen Caroline created both the Long Water (Peter Pan's statue is here) and the Serpentine by ordering the damming of the Westbourne River. Nothing so rowdy as football or cars are allowed here! Café. Park *open dawn-dusk Mon-Sun.* **Facilities**: children's playground, model boat sailing.

Primrose Hill **1 B2**

NW8. 112 acres (46.6ha) of open land. Panoramic views over London with a helpful table identifying some of the most prominent landmarks. Popular with duellists in the 19thC, the cleverest battles you'll see now are between kite-flyers. *Open 24 hrs Mon-Sun.*

Regent's Park **1 C3**

NW1. 0171-486 7905. A royal park of 472 acres (191ha), originally part of Henry VIII's great hunting forest in the 16thC. The design (1812-26) by John Nash is of great distinction. It forms two concentric circles – the Inner with gardens and the Outer with Regency terraces and imposing gateways. Here you'll find London Zoo, the Regent's Canal, a fine boating lake with more than 30 species of bird, a bandstand, fragrant flower gardens and the very fine Queen Mary's Rose Garden. Also home to the golden-domed London Central Mosque. Open-air theatre. Restaurant. Cafés. Park *open 05.00 (or dawn)-dusk Mon-Sun.* **Facilities**: athletics track, baseball, boating lake, children's playgrounds, cricket, football, rugby, tennis.

Richmond Park

Surrey 0181-948 3209. The largest of the royal parks, created by Charles I in 1632. 2358 acres (954.2ha) of natural open parkland with spinneys and plantations, bracken and ancient oaks, and over 750 red and fallow deer. Fine views of the Thames Valley from Pembroke Lodge. White Lodge was once a royal residence, now home to the Royal Ballet School. Restaurant and café in Pembroke Lodge. Park *open 07.00 (from 07.30 in winter)-½ hr before dusk Mon-Sun.* **Facilities**: children's playground, fishing (permit needed), golf, riding, polo, rugby.

St James's Park **4 E5**

SW1. 0171-930 1793. St James's is the oldest royal park, acquired by Henry VIII in 1532 and laid out in imitation 'Versailles' style by Charles II. An attractive setting, with fine promenades and walks, a romantic Chinese-style lake, bridge and weeping willows. The bird sanctuary on Duck Island has magnificent pelicans and over 20 species of duck and goose. Good views of Buckingham Palace, the domes and spires of Whitehall and, to the south, Westminster Abbey. The Mall and Constitution Hill are frequently part of royal ceremonies. Bandstand used in *summer. Open dawn-dusk Mon-Sun.*

Botanic gardens

Many parks also have living botanical collections. Holland Park has a good arboretum and others have rock gardens and extensive rose gardens, of which Queen Mary Rose Garden in Regent's Park is an outstanding example. The following provide tranquillity in the midst of London:

Chelsea Physic Garden   **6 F4**
66 Royal Hospital Rd SW3. 0171-352 5646. Founded 1673 by
the Worshipful Society of Apothecaries for the collection and
study of plants with medicinal value. Botanical research still
carried out here. Rockery made from Icelandic lava and old stone
from the Tower of London; many fine trees including the biggest
olive tree in Britain – 30ft (9.1m). *Open Apr-Oct 14.00-17.00 Wed
& 14.00-18.00 Sun. Other times by appointment only.* Charge.

Museum of Garden History   **7 F1**
Lambeth Palace Rd SE1. 0171-261 1891. 17thC garden founded at St Mary-at-Lambeth church by the Tradescants. As
gardeners to Charles I and Henrietta Maria, the father and son
team brought many rare plants into this country, some of
which can be seen in the churchyard. *Open Mar-mid Dec
10.30-16.00 Mon-Fri, 10.30-17.00 Sun. Closed Sat.* Free.

Royal Botanic Gardens, Kew
Kew Rd, Richmond, Surrey. 0181-940 1171. Superb botanic
gardens of 300 acres (121.5ha), founded in 1759 by Princess
Augusta. Within the grounds are thousands of flowers and
trees plus hot-houses for orchids, palms, ferns, cacti and
alpine plants. Lake and aquatic garden; 10-storey pagoda by
Sir William Chambers (1760); magnificent curved glass Palm
House and Temperate House (1884-8) by Decimus Burton.
The scientific aspect was developed by its two directors, Sir
William and Sir Joseph Hooker. The 17thC Queen's Garden
has a delightful herb garden and the Princess of Wales
Conservatory houses exotic plants. Beneath the Palm
House there is a Marine Display which has examples of
algae and coral reef. The new Evolution House takes you on
an expedition across thousands of millions of years. Lilac
garden. Café. Gift shop. Gardens *open from 09.30;* hot-
houses *open from 10.00. Closing times vary according to
season – phone in advance to check.* Charge.

Cemeteries

*London's cemeteries provide a fascinating insight into
Victorian attitudes with their impressive and often idiosyncratic
monuments. Originally privately owned and regimentally planted out, several have since become overgrown and peaceful
sanctuaries for wildlife.*

Brompton   **6 B4**
Old Brompton Rd SW10. Behind busy Fulham Road, vast and full
of ornamental Victorian marble tombs and memorials. Emmeline
Pankhurst, the suffragette, was buried here in 1928. Free.

Highgate
Swain's Lane N6. 0181-340 1834. Popular from the first as a
final resting place because of the good views of London from

Highgate West Hill! Winding paths lead up to The Egyptian Avenue and Cedar of Lebanon. Amongst its famous residents are Karl Marx, the writer George Eliot, the actor Sir Ralph Richardson, and the poet Christina Rossetti. Tom Sayers, the bare-fisted prizefighter, is guarded by the effigy of his mastiff who was chief mourner at his funeral and attended the ceremony in his own carriage. The conservation of the native woodland and abundance of wild flowers and birds is due to the efforts of the 'Friends of Highgate Cemetery', who offer guided tours of the West Cemetery *Apr-Oct at 12.00, 14.00 & 16.00 Mon-Fri, on the hour 11.00 16.00 Sat & Sun; Nov & Mar at 12.00, 14.00 & 15.00 Mon-Fri, on the hour 11.00-15.00 Sat & Sun. No weekday tours Dec-Feb.* Charge for tours. East Cemetery *open Apr-Oct 10.00-17.00 Mon-Fri, 11.00-17.00 Sat & Sun; Nov-Mar 10.00-16.00 Mon-Fri, 11.00-16.00 Sat & Sun.* No tours.

Kensal Green
Harrow Rd W10. 0181-969 0152. Plenty of admirable monuments and many mature native trees lining the curving avenues. Famous tombs include W.M. Thackeray and Anthony Trollope, Isambard Kingdom Brunel and his father Sir Marc Isambard Brunel, and James Miranda Barry, the Inspector General of the Army Medical Department, who on death was found to be a woman. *Open 09.00-17.30 Mon-Sat, 10.00-17.30 Sun, 10.00-13.00 Bank hols.* Free.

Walking tours

Citisights of London
213 Brooke Rd E5. 0181-806 4325. Archaeologists and historians working in association with the Museum of London provide a series of walks and tours concerning the history and archaeology of London. *Phone 0171-624 3978 to book.*

London Silver Jubilee Walkway
12-mile (19km) walkway created for the Queen's Silver Jubilee in 1977. Circles the centre of London, passing close to many famous and historic buildings. Start at Leicester Square (**4 E3**) and follow the discs set in the pavement. Leaflet obtainable from the London Tourist Board Information Centre, Victoria Station Forecourt SW1 (**7 B2**).

The *Original* London Walks
PO Box 1708 NW6. 0171-624 3978. A choice of more than 40 walks lasting about *2 hrs* including Dickens' London, Ghosts of the City and Jack the Ripper haunts. Also pub walks. *Mon-Sun; first walk 10.30, last walk 19.30.* **Meeting place**: *usually at a tube station. Phone for further details.* Charge.

Streets of London
16 The Grove N3. 0181-346 9255. Guided walking tours with a
regular programme of scheduled tours, regardless of weather.
Themes include Dickens' London and History of London.
Meeting place: *usually at a tube station. Phone for further
details.* Charge.

Coach tours

Evan Evans   **4 E4**
26 Cockspur St SW1. 0171-930 2377. Well-established tour
company which operates a variety of tours; *full day, morning*
or *afternoon* plus a *2½-hr* general drive around the capital and a
30-min cruise on the Thames. Also run extended tours out of
London.
Harrods   **3 G6**
Sightseeing Tours Dept, Harrods, Knightsbridge SW1. 0171-
581 3603. The most luxurious coach tour of London; takes
2 hrs with a taped commentary in several languages and
refreshments on board. Also an all-day London tour which
includes a 3-course lunch. Tours to Stratford-upon-Avon and
Blenheim Palace.
Original London Sightseeing Tours
London Coaches, Jew's Row SW18. 0181-877 1722. Round
London tours in traditional double-decker buses, some of
which are open-topped. A great favourite with children. *Phone
for further details.*

River trips and tours

*One of the best ways to appreciate London is to take a boat
trip. The Thames is a fascinatingly beautiful river, particularly
as it passes through the city, where the buildings lining its
banks conjure up a whole host of historic, artistic and literary
associations. There are several companies running river and
canal trips.*
*The London Tourist Board provides an excellent River Trips
telephone information service on (0839) 123432 (recorded
information).*
NB: always check times of return boats at the pier on arrival.

DOWNRIVER SERVICES
Charing Cross Pier   **4 F4**
Victoria Embankment WC2. 0171-839 3572. Trips to the
Tower *(20 mins)* and Greenwich *(45 mins) Apr-Oct every half
hour between 10.30-16.00 Mon-Sun; Nov-Mar every 45 mins
between 10.30-15.00 Mon-Sun. 2-hr luncheon cruise 12.45
Sun only; all year.*

Greenwich Pier
Return services to Charing Cross Pier *(45 mins)*, Tower Pier *(½ hr)* and Westminster Pier *(45 mins)*. *Phone the individual piers for details.*

Tower Pier   5 F4
0171-488 0344. Trips to Westminster *(25 mins) every 20 mins 11.00-18.00 in summer (every 40 mins 11.00-17.00 Nov-Mar).* Ferry to *HMS Belfast (5 mins) every 15 mins in summer only.*

Westminster Pier   4 F5
Victoria Embankment WC2. 0171-930 4097. Trips to the Tower *(½ hr) every 20 mins 10.30-16.00* and to Greenwich *(50 mins) every half hour 10.30-16.00; all year.* Special trips to the Thames Flood Barrier *(1¼ hrs each way) 10.00, 11.15, 12.45, 13.45 & 15.15 Mar-Nov.* Disco cruises *19.00 Fri & 20.00 Sat in summer.*

UPRIVER SERVICES
Westminster Pier   4 F5
Victoria Embankment SW1. Westminster Passenger Services operate boat trips *during summer only* to Putney *(½ hr)*, Kew *(1½ hrs)*, Richmond *(2 hrs)* and Hampton Court *(3-4 hrs). Phone 0171-930 2062 for departure times.*

There are local services to Hampton Court from Richmond and Kingston *(Easter-Sep). Phone 0181-546 2434 for details.*

UPPER THAMES
Salter Bros
Follybridge, Oxford. (01865) 243421. Salter's steamers run from Oxford-Abingdon, Reading-Henley, Maidenhead-Windsor and Windsor-Staines; *May-Sep Mon-Sun. Phone for details.*

Canal trips

Canal Water Bus   1 D1
London Waterbus Company, Camden Lock Place NW1. 0171-482 2550. Boats leave from Little Venice, stopping at London Zoo and continuing to Camden Lock; *Apr-Oct 10.00-17.00 Mon-Sun.* Also run Limehouse/River Lea trips which explore the architecture and industrial history of London's quiet canalways; *May-Sep 09.30-18.00 Sat. Phone for details of departure times.*

Jason's Trip   3 C1
opposite 60 Blomfield Rd W9. 0171-286 3428. The traditional narrowboat *Jason* leaves Little Venice for a *1½-hr* return trip with commentary, through Regent's Park (with London Zoo) to Camden Lock. Disembark to look round the craft shops if you like, or the market at *weekends*. Refreshments and lunch available. *Phone for details of departure times.*

Jenny Wren Cruises **1 D1**
250 Camden High St NW1. 0171-485 4433. *Jenny Wren*, a traditional canal boat, goes from Camden Lock to Little Venice without stopping. The round trip takes *1½ hrs*. Trips run from *Feb-Nov four times a day Mon-Sun. Phone for details of departure times.*

Zoos, safari parks and fun days out

Bekonscot Model Village
Warwick Rd, Beaconsfield, Bucks. (01494) 672919. 23 miles/37km west (A40, M40). Miniature wonderland set in the 1930s, created by Roland Callingham. A raised viewing platform offers a bird's eye view of the miniature world of shops, streets and inhabitants, but the real home pride of Bekonscot is the model (gauge 1) railway which travels round the village. *Open Mar-Oct 10.00-17.00 Mon-Sun.* Charge.

Birdworld & Underwater World
Holt Pound, Farnham, Surrey. (01420) 22140. 30 miles/48km south west (A3, A31). Situated on the edge of Alice Holt Forest, there are beautiful gardens here which make the perfect home for a huge variety of birds from the tiny humming bird to the huge ostrich. Watch the pelicans catch fish in their beaks or feeding time at Penguin Island. There are good, well laid-out trails. **Underwater World** is next door, with a large indoor aquarium full of amazing colourful tropical fish. Both *open Apr-Aug 09.30-18.00 Mon-Sun; Sep 09.30-17.00 Mon-Sun; Oct-Mar 09.30-16.00 Mon-Sun.* Charge.

Chessington World of Adventures
Leatherhead Rd, Chessington, Surrey. (01372) 727227. 12 miles/19km south (A3, A243). 65 acres (27ha) comprising a zoo and theme park with wild rides such as Terror Tomb and The Vampire – Britain's first hanging roller coaster. Visit the Mystic East, Circus World and Toytown. A monorail travels high above the zoo animals. All attractions *open mid Mar-Oct 10.00-17.00 Mon-Sun*; zoo only *open Nov-Mar 10.00-16.00 Mon-Sun.* Charge.

Chislehurst Caves
Old Hill, Chislehurst, Kent. 0181-467 3264. 12 miles/19km south east (A2, A20, A222). A maze of chalk tunnels and caves, created in the stone ages. The caves have been inhabited in the past by druids, the Romans and Londoners seeking shelter during the air raids of World War II. Go on one of the eerie lamplight guided tours. They last *45 mins* and leave *every half hour*. On *Sun and Bank hols* there is a *1½-hr* tour which leaves at *14.30*. *Open 11.00-16.30 Mon-Sun.* Charge.

Cotswold Wildlife Park

Burford, Oxon. (01993) 823006. 75 miles/120km west (M40, A40). Large and varied collection of animals can be seen in natural surroundings. Rhinos, zebras and ostriches roam in large paddocks bounded by unobtrusive moats. More dangerous species, such as leopards, are caged. Adventure playground and farmyard where tame animals can be stroked. Narrow gauge railway operates *during summer*. Restaurant. Brass rubbing centre. *Open 10.00-18.00 (or dusk) Mon-Sun*. Charge.

London Zoo   1 C3

Regent's Park NW1. 0171-722 3333. Famous zoo with a strong conservation and breeding policy. Aviary designed by Lord Snowdon. 'Moonlight World' reverses day and night so that rarely-seen nocturnal animals are kept awake during the day. *Open Apr-Oct 10.00-17.30 Mon-Sun; Nov-Mar 10.00-dusk Mon-Sun. Closed Xmas Day.* Charge (includes admittance to London Aquarium).

Thorpe Park

Staines Rd, Chertsey, Surrey. (01932) 562633. 21 miles/34km south west (A308). A wonderful place for all ages, with lots of rides and entertainments such as Flying Fish and Thunder River. Thorpe Farm is good for small children. All rides covered by entrance fee. *Open end Mar-Jun 10.00-17.00 Mon-Sun; Jul-Sep 10.00-18.00 Mon-Sun; Oct 10.00-17.00; (last admission 2 hours before closing time). Closed Nov-end Mar.* Charge (children under 1 metre tall free!).

Whipsnade Wild Animal Park

Dunstable, Beds. (01582) 872171. 32 miles/51km north (M1, A5). Natural zoo of woods and downland with over 2500 animals in large open-air enclosures. Some species roam freely. Travel round the park by car or aboard the trailbreaker road train. Also a Discovery Centre with hands-on displays, a miniature desert and wall-to-wall rainforests. *Open Apr-Oct 10.00-dusk Mon-Sun; Nov-Mar 10.00-16.00 Mon-Sun.* Charge.

Woburn Safari Park

Woburn, Beds. (01525) 290407. 40 miles/64km north (M1). Britain's largest drive-through safari park. A winding route takes you past tigers, bears, wolves, rhinos and mischievous monkeys! At the end of the safari trail you can watch sealion and parrot shows. Wild World Leisure Area with rides, boating lake and cable car. 3000-acre (1250ha) park surrounding Woburn Abbey contains original herd of Père David deer. *Open Mar-end Oct 10.00-17.00 Mon-Sun; Nov-Feb 11.00-15.00 Sat & Sun.* Charge.

Stately homes

Arundel Castle

Arundel, W. Sussex. (01903) 882173. 58 miles/93km south (A24, A29). Once an imposing feudal stronghold overlooking the River Arun. Home to the Dukes of Norfolk for 700 years. Magnificent collection of paintings by van Dyck, Holbein and Gainsborough. *Open Apr-Oct 11.00-17.00 Mon-Fri & Sun (closed Sat). Closed Nov-Mar. Last admission 1 hour before closing time.* Charge.

Blenheim Palace

Woodstock, Oxon. (01993) 811325. 60 miles/96km west (M40, A34). Birthplace of Sir Winston Churchill. Huge palace built 1705-22 by Sir John Vanbrugh. Fine example of English baroque architecture. Now home to the 11th Duke of Marlborough. Fine tapestries, sculpture and furnishings. *Open mid Mar-Oct 10.30-17.30 Mon-Sun. Closed Nov-mid Mar.* Charge. Landscaped park *open 09.00-17.00 Mon-Sun all year.*

Goodwood

nr Chichester, W. Sussex. (01243) 774107. 60 miles/96km south (A3, A283, then A285 or A286). 18thC house by James Wyatt. Home to the 10th Duke of Richmond. Superb artistic connections, with masterpieces by Canaletto, van Dyck, Kneller and Reynolds. Fine examples of French furniture, Sèvres porcelain and Gobelins tapestries. House often used for entertainment functions. Aerodrome and famous motor circuit nearby. Has its own race-course, where 'Glorious Goodwood', a famous meet, takes place at the *end of Jul.* Advisable to phone in advance as there is *no public access on event days. Open May-Sep 14.00-17.00 Sun & Mon (also open 14.00-17.00 Tue-Thur in Aug); open Easter Sun & Mon. Closed on event days.* Charge.

Hatfield House

Hatfield, Herts. (01707) 262823. 21 miles/34km north (A1, A1000). Jacobean mansion built 1611 for Robert Cecil, 1st Earl of Salisbury. Still home to the Cecil family. Famous portraits, rare tapestries, fine furniture and armour. Tudor Old Royal Palace in grounds, where Queen Elizabeth I learned of her accession to the throne. Beautiful grounds with woodlands and lake. *Open (guided tours only) end Mar-Oct 12.00-17.00 Tue-Sat (last tour 16.00). Closed Mon except Bank hols; open 11.00-17.00 (no guided tours). Closed Nov-end Mar.* Charge. Park *open 10.30-20.00 daily.*

Leeds Castle

Maidstone, Kent. (01622) 765400. 40 miles/64km south east

(A20, M20). Beautiful, romantic, restored castle (AD 857). Magnificent collection of medieval furnishings, French and English fabrics, tapestries and paintings by Degas, Pissarro and Vuillard. Delightful gardens. Shop, licensed restaurant, garden centre. *Open Mar-Oct 10.00-17.00 Mon-Sun; Nov-Feb 10.00-15.00 Mon-Sun (last admission 1 hour before closing time).* Charge.

Royal Pavilion, Brighton

Old Steine, Brighton, E. Sussex. (01273) 603005. 45 miles/72km south (A23). Fantastic Oriental seaside 'villa' with onion domes and minarets built for the Prince Regent (later George IV) by Nash 1815-22. Lavish Chinese-style state rooms. *Open Jun-Sep 10.00-18.00 Mon-Sun; Oct-May 10.00-17.00 Mon-Sun.* Charge.

Windsor Castle

Windsor, Berks. (01753) 868286. 20 miles/32km west (M4). Imposing 800-year-old medieval fortress adjoining nearly 5000 acres of home park and gardens. 12thC Round Tower built by Henry II; St George's Chapel fine example of 16thC perpendicular. Castle precinct and state apartments. *Opening times depend on the movements of the royal family and ceremonial occasions, so check with the Castle Information Office.* Charge.

Woburn Abbey

Woburn, Beds. (01525) 290666. 40 miles/64km north (M1). Home of Dukes of Bedford for over 300 years. Built on the site of a Cistercian monastery, founded 1145. Present building dates from 17thC and 18thC. Set in 3000-acre deer park, part of which is now a safari park (see page 56). Collection of paintings includes works by Rembrandt, Gainsborough, Holbein and Canaletto. *Open Jan-Mar 11.00-16.00 Sat & Sun; Apr-Oct 11.00-16.00 Mon-Sun. Closed Nov & Dec.* Charge.

Day trips

The telephone numbers listed in the following entries refer to the Tourist Information Centre in the town. ⇌ refers to the British Rail station for that destination.

Bath

107 miles/171km west (M4, A4). ⇌ : Paddington. (01225) 462831. Elegant Georgian town, rich in architectural detail. See the dramatic sweeping curve of Ionic columns forming the Royal Crescent. Several museums including Roman Baths with natural hot springs, from which the town got its name and indeed its existence. Good shops.

Brighton
56 miles/90km south (A23). ⇌: Victoria. (01273) 323755. Originally a poor fishing village which became fashionable when the Royal Pavilion was built here (see page 58). Splendid Regency terraces, five miles of beach and interesting shops in The Lanes; unusual jewellery, antiques, clothes and artefacts. The restored Victorian pier is full of attractions. Marina has waterside pubs and cafés.

Cambridge
60 miles/96km north (M11). ⇌: King's Cross. (01223) 322640. University city of spires, mellow colleges and riverside meadows, bordering the River Cam. Hire a punt to view the university colleges and serene lawns. 31 colleges in total; the oldest, Peterhouse, was established in 1284. King's College Chapel is one of the world's Gothic masterpieces. The Fitzwilliam Museum has a superb collection of classical antiquities and paintings.

Henley-on-Thames
Oxon. 36 miles/57km west (A4). ⇌: Paddington. (01491) 578034. Situated on a very pretty part of the Thames and most famous for the Regatta, held in *early Jul* (see page 36). Arched bridge was built in 1786. In St Mary's churchyard are 16thC almshouses and a rare unspoilt 15thC timber-framed building – the Chantry House. The Regatta is held on the straight mile of river downstream from the bridge.

Oxford
56 miles/90km west (M40). ⇌: Paddington. (01865) 726871. A University city of 'dreaming spires' and fine college buildings. 30 colleges, all worth a visit – the grandest being Christ Church and the oldest University College (1249). Other attractions include the Sheldonian Theatre by Wren, the 15thC Bodleian Library, the Ashmolean Museum, and the oldest botanic gardens in Britain. In addition there are several good pubs and restaurants.

Stratford-on-Avon
Warks. 90 miles/144km north west (M40, A34). ⇌: Liverpool Street. (01789) 293127. The birthplace of William Shakespeare (1564-1616). The town is still Elizabethan in atmosphere, with overhanging gables and timbered inns. Visit the writer's birthplace in Henley Street, his house at New Place, Anne Hathaway's cottage and the museum and picture gallery. The Shakespeare Memorial Theatre in Waterside is thriving and progressive.

SHOPPING

See page 126 for a map of the main shopping streets in London. For shop-by-shop street maps see pp68-75.
Generally shops open 09.00/10.00-17.30/18.00 Mon-Sat and are closed on Sun & Bank hols, though many do now open on Sun. Many Bond Street shops do not open on Sat. In cases where a shop's hours differ from the standard times above, the opening hours appear in italic at the end of the entry. Some areas have a late shopping night. See individual shopping areas below.

Tax free shopping

Most goods and services in the UK are subject to VAT (value added tax) at the standard rate of 17½%. Luxury items – such as tobacco, perfume, alcoholic beverages and motor vehicles – are subject to higher rates. A good way to purchase tax-free goods is to shop in stores showing the London Tax Free Shopping sign. This system entails filling in a voucher, presenting it to customs with the goods and returning it to the London Tax Free Shopping organisation which will then immediately refund your money in the currency of your country of residence.

Shopping areas

Camden   1 D2
A popular and trendy canalside area lined with shops and a huge, sprawling market. Come here if you're looking for period clothes, alternative books, imported records, pine furniture and artefacts. It's at its busiest and liveliest on *Sat & Sun afternoons.*

Covent Garden   4 F3
Once the site of the famous fruit and vegetable market, this is now a fashionable pedestrianised piazza. The arcades are lined with small specialist fashion and gift shops, plus plenty of places to eat and drink. There are also open-air craft stalls, an antiques market and an occasional craft market. Leading off the piazza in every direction, the streets reveal an interesting variety of shops and restaurants with the latest in fashion, high-tech household equipment and exotic foods. *Late night Thur.* Many shops *open late Mon-Sat* and *all day Sun.*

Kensington High Street 3 B6
Less hectic than Oxford Street, though a similar range of shops and large branches of most high street chains, plus Barkers of Kensington, its own department store. Delve into the roads leading off for more individual (and more expensive) fashion shops. *Late night Thur.*

King's Road/Chelsea 6 E3
One of the centres for up-to-the-minute fashion, plus high street chains, it is particularly good for shoes and men's clothing. *Late night Wed.*

Knightsbridge 3 G5
A traditionally fashionable area for the rich and famous, dominated by Harrods and Harvey Nichols. Beauchamp Place also has exclusive furniture, jewellery and clothes. *Late night Wed.*

Piccadilly/Trocadero/London Pavilion 4 E3
Quality and tradition in the form of Fortnum & Mason, Hatchards, Simpson, and Lillywhites. Also the historic Burlington Arcade. The Trocadero and London Pavilion cater for the more up-to-date taste with one-stop shopping, refreshment and entertainment, while Tower Records dominates Piccadilly Circus from the old Swan & Edgar building. Many shops *open late Mon-Sat.*

Soho 4 E2
Cosmopolitan Soho is an excellent location for specialist shopping. International food shops, oriental supermarkets, and designer clothes. Also trendy restaurants and bars. Berwick Street Market and Chinatown both merit a visit.

West End
London's biggest shopping area consisting of three main streets. **Oxford Street** (**4 C2**) is over a mile long and has nearly all the major department stores including Selfridges, John Lewis, London's largest Marks & Spencer and an overwhelming assortment of individual fashion shops. It gets very crowded here, especially on *Sat* and at *lunchtime*. **Regent Street** (**4 D3**) is less hectic and offers luxurious items and gifts from Liberty, plus several china, glass and clothing stores and the department store Dickins & Jones. **Carnaby Street** (**4 D3**) is still worth a visit. World-renowned in the 1960s, it has retained its busy and lively atmosphere, with frequent pavement shows and interesting clothes and souvenir shops. Some of the high street chains have now also moved in. For real luxury try **New Bond Street** (**4 C3**) where you'll find shoes, jewellery, prints, pictures and designer clothes. Two pedestrianised streets just off Oxford Street, and well worth exploring, are **St Christopher's Place** (**4 B2**) and **South Molton Street** (**4 C2**). Both are packed with stylish small shops and attractive eating places. *Late night Thur.*

Whiteleys   3 C3
Queensway W2. One of the first department stores, now transformed into a smart, cosmopolitan complex of shops, cafés, restaurants, bars and an eight-screen cinema. Many shops *open late Mon-Sat.*

Department stores

Army & Navy   7 C1
101-105 Victoria St SW1. 0171-834 1234. Excellent food hall and wine department. Clothing, cosmetics, household goods, toys, books, china and glass. Hairdressing salon. Coffee shop. Restaurant. *Open 09.30-18.00 Mon-Sat (to 18.30 Thur & Fri).*

Barkers of Kensington   3 C5
63 Kensington High St W8. 0171-937 5432. Fashionable clothes, household and electrical goods and a hairdressing/beauty salon. Restaurant. Café. *Open 10.00-18.30 Mon-Fri (to 19.00 Thur), 09.30-18.30 Sat.*

BHS (British Home Stores)   4 C2
252 Oxford St W1. 0171-629 2011. Inexpensive clothes and accessories for men, women and children. Household goods and extensive lighting department. Restaurant. *Open 09.00-19.00 Mon-Sat (to 20.00 Thur).*

Debenhams   4 D2
344-348 Oxford St W1. 0171-580 3000. Fashion clothes at reasonable prices. Good kitchenware, lingerie, hosiery and cosmetics departments. Restaurant. *Open 09.00-19.00 Mon & Tue, 10.00-20.00 Wed, 09.30-20.00 Thur & Fri, 09.30-19.00 Sat.*

D.H. Evans   4 D2
318 Oxford St W1. 0171-629 8800. Part of the House of Fraser group with excellent fashion and lingerie departments. Unusual sizes are well catered for in the dress department. Also perfumery, furniture and household goods. Olympus Sports is in the basement. Restaurant. Café. *Open 10.00-18.30 Mon-Fri (to 20.00 Thur), 09.00-19.00 Sat.*

Dickins & Jones   4 D3
224 Regent St W1. 0171-734 7070. Fashionable store selling stylish ladies' and men's clothes, accessories and haberdashery. Excellent and wide range of dress fabrics. Also china and glass departments. Hairdressers. Beauty salon. Restaurant. Coffee shop. *Open 09.30-18.30 Mon-Sat (to 20.00 Thur).*

Fenwick   4 C3
63 New Bond St W1. 0171-629 9161. Good fashions and accessories. Imaginative gifts and stationery and a wide selection of books. *Open 09.30-18.00 Mon-Sat (to 19.30 Thur).*

Fortnum & Mason   4 D4
181 Piccadilly W1. 0171-734 8040. Well-established and

respected store. Famous for its exotic foods, but also offers jewellery, china, glass, fashion, perfumery, leather goods, toys, stationery and a beauty salon. Three restaurants. *Open 09.30-18.00 Mon-Sat.*

Harrods   **3 G6**
Knightsbridge SW1. 0171-730 1234. The world's most famous department store – over 60 fashion departments with men's, ladies' and children's clothing and accessories. Also perfumes, gifts, china, glass, pets, toys, books, furniture and fabrics. The Edwardian marble food halls are well worth a visit for their luxury foods. Wide range of services. Bureau de change. Barber's shop. Hairdressers. Beauty salon. Six restaurants. Three coffee shops. *Open 10.00-18.00 Mon, Tue & Sat, 10.00-19.00 Wed, Thur & Fri.*

Harvey Nichols   **4 A5**
Knightsbridge SW1. 0171-235 5000. Elegant, stylish clothes from top British, Continental and American designers. Home furnishings and household goods. Restaurant. *Open 10.00-19.00 Mon-Fri (to 20.00 Wed), to 18.00 Sat.*

Heal's/Habitat   **4 E1**
196 Tottenham Court Rd W1. 0171-631 3880. Terence Conran's brainchild – Habitat offers affordable furniture, kitchenware, rugs, stationery, posters. Heal's is more expensive with more unusual designs and gift ideas. Restaurant in Heal's. *Open 10.00-18.00 Mon-Wed, to 20.00 Thur, to 18.30 Fri & Sat, 12.00-17.30 Sun.*

John Lewis   **4 C2**
278-306 Oxford St W1. 0171-629 7711. One of the largest dress fabric departments in Europe, as well as furniture, furnishings, china, glass, household goods and fashions. Excellent haberdashery department. Bureau de change. Interpreters available. NB: They do not take credit cards. Restaurant. Coffee shop. Other branches. *Open 09.00-17.30 Mon-Sat (09.30-20.00 Thur).*

Liberty   **4 D3**
210-220 Regent St W1. 0171-734 1234. Famous and fashionable, well-known for distinctive fabrics and unusual luxury goods. Good selection of unusual jewellery and rare gifts, plus glass, china, oriental rugs, prints, gifts and several designer-label collections. Restaurant. Coffee shop. *Open 09.30-18.00 Mon-Sat (to 19.30 Thur).*

Littlewoods   **4 B2**
508-520 Oxford St W1. 0171-629 7847. Inexpensive high street chain for clothing and household goods. *Open 09.00-19.00 Mon-Sat (to 20.00 Thur).*

Marks & Spencer   **4 B2**
458 Oxford St W1. 0171-935 7954. Well-loved chain with good quality inexpensive clothing and accessories for men, women

and children. Wide range of foods, home furnishings, cosmetics and gifts. Other branches. Bureau de change. NB: They do not take credit cards. *Open 09.00-19.00 Mon-Wed & Sat, to 20.00 Thur & Fri.*

Peter Jones **6 F2**

Sloane Sq SW1. 0171-730 3434. (Part of same chain as John Lewis.) Excellent quality and good value clothing, accessories and household goods. Also modern and antique furniture, glass, china, and a large furnishing fabric department. Interpreters available. Restaurant. Coffee shop. NB: They do not take credit cards. *Open 09.00-17.30 Mon-Sat (09.30-19.00 Wed).*

Selfridges **4 B2**

400 Oxford St W1. 0171-629 1234. Vast store with huge range of clothing, accessories and household goods. Also toys, sports clothing and equipment and an impressive food hall. Three restaurants. Five cafés. *Open 09.30-19.00 Mon-Sat (to 20.00 Thur).*

Clothes stores

See page 76 for a clothing size conversion chart.

Nearly all London's department stores have extensive collections of clothes and accessories, but these are the specialists:

Aquascutum **4 D3**

100 Regent St W1. 0171-734 6090. Fine quality British rain coats, suits, knitwear and accessories for men and women.

Austin Reed **4 D3**

103-113 Regent St W1. 0171-734 6789. English and Continental suits and accessories for men. Accent on quality. Valet service and barber. Also ladies' clothing, executive suits, designer wear and classic dresses.

Burberrys **4 E3**

18-22 Haymarket SW1. 0171-930 3343. Classic raincoats for men and women cut in the English style. Hats, scarves, suits and accessories. Other branches.

C&A **4 B2**

501-509 Oxford St W1. 0171-629 7272. Vast selection of reasonably priced fashions and classics for all the family including skirts, dresses, coats, knitwear, suits and leathers. Clockhouse is for 14-25 year-olds. Good selection of sports clothing, especially ski wear. Other branches. *Open 09.30-18.00 Mon-Sat (to 20.00 Thur).*

Jaeger **4 D3**

200-206 Regent St W1. 0171-734 8211. Four floors of well-cut, classic clothes. Suits, coats, knitwear and casual wear for men; dresses, suits and separates for women in colour co-ordinated departments. Accessories, jewellery. Other branches.

Lillywhites   **4 E3**
Piccadilly Circus W1. 0171-930 3181. Five floors of sports clothing and equipment for just about any sport you can think of.

Moss Bros   **4 F3**
27-29 King St WC2. 0171-240 4567. Men's ceremonial and formal wear. Morning suits, dinner jackets, bow ties, top hat and tails, accessories. Arrange hire at least one week in advance. Deposit required. Other branches.

Next   **4 C2**
327-329 Oxford St W1. 0171-409 2746. Fashions for men and women. Also cosmetics, lingerie, accessories, flowers and home furnishings. Other branches.

Simpson   **4 D4**
203 Piccadilly W1. 0171-734 2002. High-quality clothing for men and women. Shirts, knitwear, dresses and separates. Daks country clothes, luggage and accessories. Restaurant.

Antiques

Good hunting grounds are the King's Road, Portobello Road, Camden Passage in Islington, Kensington Church Street, Fulham Road and Camden Town.

Antiquarius   **6 E3**
137 King's Rd SW3. 0171-352 7989. Over 150 stalls with clothing, jewellery, china, glass, books and prints.

Chelsea Antiques Market   **6 E4**
245-253 King's Rd SW3. 0171-352 5581. Large, busy market – mainly books, jewellery, glass, china.

Gallery of Antique Costume & Textiles
2 Church St NW8. 0171-723 9981. Suppliers of antique costumes and textiles including clothing and fabrics from all over the world. Reasonable prices.

Grays Antiques Market   **4 C3**
1-7 Davies Mews W1. 0171-629 7034. London's busiest antiques centre with over 250 dealers. Huge selection of antiques and collectables.

Auctioneers

W.& F.C. Bonham & Sons   **3 F6**
Montpelier Galleries, Montpelier St SW7. 0171-584 9161. Paintings, furniture, carpets, porcelain, jewellery and silver. Branch: 65-69 Lots Rd SW10 (**6 C5**). 0171-351 7111.

Christie's   **4 D4**
8 King St SW1. 0171-839 9060. Internationally famous. Comprehensive fine art auctioneers since 1766. Branch: 85 Old Brompton Rd SW7 (**6 D2**). 0171-581 7611.

Sotheby's   **4 C3**
34-35 New Bond St W1. 0171-493 8080. Internationally
famous for antiques and works of art. Paintings, ceramics,
glass, furniture, silver, jewellery, books and manuscripts.

Books

Books etc   **4 E2**
120 Charing Cross Rd WC2. 0171-379 6838. General book-
store. Other branches.

Dillons   **1 F6**
82 Gower St W1. 0171-636 1577. Vast stock of paperbacks
and hardbacks with large academic range. Other branches.
Open 09.00-19.00 Mon-Fri, to 18.00 Sat.

Foyles   **4 E2**
119-125 Charing Cross Rd WC2. 0171-437 5660. London's
largest book store with practically every English book in print.

Hatchards   **4 D4**
187 Piccadilly W1. 0171-439 9921. Something of an institution
with a comprehensive selection of general books and
knowledgeable staff. Other branches.

W.H. Smith   **6 F2**
36 Sloane Sq SW1. 0171-730 0351. Well-known retailer, with
a wide choice of books, magazines, stationery, records, tapes,
CDs and games. Many other branches.

Waterstone's   **3 C5**
193 Kensington High St W8. 0171-937 8432. Excellent general
store with comprehensive selections in just about every
subject you can think of. Other branches. *Open 09.30-21.00
Mon-Fri, to 19.00 Sat, 11.00-18.00 Sun.*

Crafts

Contemporary Applied Arts   **4 F2**
43 Earlham St WC2. 0171-836 6993. Comprehensive display
of work by craftsmen using a variety of materials.

Naturally British   **4 F3**
13 New Row WC2. 0171-240 0551. High-quality hand-made
British goods including pottery, toys, clothes and jewellery.

Food

*Fortnum & Mason, Harrods and Selfridges have particularly
impressive food halls. The following are more specialist shops:*

H.R. Higgins   **4 D4**
79 Duke St W1. 0171-629 3913. Over 40 types of coffee
including original and blended, light, medium and dark roasts.

Partridges   **6 F2**
132-134 Sloane St SW1. 0171-730 0651. Delightful, well-

established shop with exquisite fruits and vegetables, unusual canned and tinned provisions.

Paxton & Whitfield **4 D4**
93 Jermyn St W1. 0171-930 0259. Over 250 superb English and Continental cheeses plus traditional hams, home-made pies and pâtés.

Gifts

Crabtree & Evelyn **3 B4**
6 Kensington Church St W8. 0171-937 9335. Exquisite perfumes and toiletries for men and women. All beautifully packaged. *Open 09.30-18.00 Mon-Sat (to 19.00 Thur).*

General Trading Company **6 F2**
144 Sloane St SW1. 0171-730 0411. Some of the best designs in contemporary English and Continental glass and china. Café. *Open 09.00-17.30 Mon-Sat (to 19.00 Wed).*

Past Times **6 E1**
146 Brompton Rd SW3. 0171-581 7616. Reproduction jewellery, crafts and cards from 4000 years of British history. Curiosities and books.

Markets

Berwick Street **4 E2**
W1. Busy and boisterous general market in the heart of Soho since 1892. Good value fruit and vegetables; also meat, cheeses, fresh fish and household goods. *Open 09.00-18.00 Mon-Sat.*

Camden Lock **1 D1**
Where Chalk Farm Rd crosses Regent's Canal NW1. Among the cobbled courtyards and warehouses of the lock is a huge market area selling everything from designer clothes and pine furniture to antique clothing and junk. Also interesting food stalls. *Open 08.00-18.00 Mon-Sun.*

Petticoat Lane **5 F1**
The name given to the market radiating from Middlesex Street. Probably named after the second-hand clothes dealers who had their businesses here in the early 1600s. Lively and hectic, with mainly clothing on sale, but also toys, food, toiletries and luxury goods. *Open 09.00-14.00 Sun only.*

Portobello Road **3 A2**
W11. Well-known and much-frequented market extending into Golborne Road and Westbourne Grove. Fruit, vegetables and new goods sold *07.00-18.00 Mon-Sat. Closed Thur.* Second-hand junk and bric-à-brac sold *08.00-17.00 Fri,* and the famous antiques market is held *08.00-17.00 Sat.*

Oxford Street

Tottenham Court Road				**Charing Cross Road**
Fashion M **Hornes**	4		7	**Morgan** Fashion F
Pub **The Tottenham**	6		6	Tottenham Court Road
Restaurant **McDonald's**	8		15	**K Shoes** Shoes FM
Sock Shop	10		17	**Wigwam** Gifts
Mecca Entertainment & Catering	12		19	Regent School of Languages
Records **Virgin Megastore**	14		19	**Challoner** Employment agency
MGM Cinema	16		19	**Dillons** Books
Fashion M **Harmony**	20		25	Office Angels Employment agency
Comics & books **Virgin**	22		25	**Messrs C** Foods
Foodstore **7-Eleven**	24		29	**Pizza Hut** Restaurant
Records, CDs & cassettes **Virgin Megastore**	26		33	**Nick Nack** Gifts
Sotheby's Library & Educational Services	30		35	**Papagallo's** Take-away food
Lloyds Bank	32		37	**Ryman** Stationery
Shoes FM **Barratts**	36		41	**Cardshops** Cards & posters
Fashion FM **Jeans West**	38		45	**Sightcare** Opticians
Fashion FM **Academy**	44		45	Mayfair School of English
Leather goods **Eternité**	46		47	Key Employment agency
Restaurant **Angus Steak House**	48		47	**Sonico Jeans Centre** Fashion FM
			49	**Outlet 49** Fashion M
			49	Kelly Employment agency
			51	**The Bootstore**
Hanway Street			53	**Mondo Pelle** Leather fashion
			55	**Suits You** Fashion M
Shoes M **Footsie 100**	50			
Midland Bank	52			**Soho Street**
Rathbone Place			61	**Ratners** Jewellers
			63	Chequepoint Bureau de change
Restaurant **Piet a Manger**	56		65	LIA Amusement Arcade
Fashion FM **Lace**	58		67	**CJ's** Fashion M
Building society **Halifax**	60		73	**Mash** Fashion M
Natural beauty products **The Body Shop**	66		75	**The Knockout Clothing Store** Fashion FM
Travel goods **Salisburys**	68a		79	**79 Club** Nightclub
			83	**Toro Leather Wear** Fashion FM
Perry's Place			85	**Marmalade** Fashion F
			87	**Pizza Hut** Restaurant
Hi-fi **McDonalds Electronics**	70		89	**Sock Shop**
Newsagent, gifts & cards **Oxford News**	78			
CDs **Buzzz**	80			**Dean Street**
Shoes FM **Dolcis**	82			
Cameras & electronics **Dixons**	86		91	**Tie Rack** Fashion FM
			93	**Knickerbox** Underwear
			95	**Eurochange** Bureau de change
			97	**Woodhouse** Fashion M
			101	**Best of London** Souvenirs
Newman Street				
				Great Chapel Street
Opticians **Eyeland – Dolland & Aitchison**	92		103	**Slot Machine** Fashion FM
Chemist **Boots**	94		109	**Mark-One** Fashion F
Zone Games Centre	100		111	**Cobra** Sports goods
Nightclub **100 Club**	100		113	**Bust Clothing Company** Fashion FM
Fashion F **Stirling Cooper**	104		115	**Warrior** Fashion M
Gifts **Extra**	112		117	**Athena** Posters, cards, gifts
National Westminster Bank	112		117	**Claude Gill** Books
			123	**Holland & Barrett** Health foodstore
			125	**Benetton** Fashion F
Berners Street				
				Wardour Street
Fashion F **Principles**	114			
Fashion M **High & Mighty**	116		129	**Clearance Depot** Clearance store
Fashion FM **Tie Rack**	118		129	**Trio Crest** Clearance store
SHOPPING CENTRE **THE PLAZA**			137	**Footsie 100** Shoes FM
Fashion FM **The Gap**	124		139	Callan School of English
			141	**Rush Me** Fashion F
Wells Street				
				Berwick Street
Sportswear **Olympus**	134			
Fashion M **Mister Byrite**	140		145	**J. D. Sports** Sportswear
Restaurant **Burger King**	142		145	Accountants on Call Employment agency
Novelties, cards **Surprise**	146		147	**Sacha** Shoes FM
Employment agency Action Secretary	146		149	**Jeans West** Fashion FM
Records **HMV Shop**	150		151	**Boots** Chemist
Fashion M **Oakland**	156		153	**Jane Norman** Fashion F
Fashion FM **California Jeans**	158		155	**The Sale** Fashion F
Fashion M **Profile**	160		159	**Shellys** Shoes
Fashion M **The State of Independence**	162			
				Poland Street
			163	**Books Etc** Books
			165	Abbey National Building society
			167	**H.Samuel** Jewellers
			173	**MARKS & SPENCER** STORE
			175	**Saxone** Shoes FM
			181	Next Employment agency
			181	**Dolcis** Shoes FM
			185	Ecco Recruitment consultants
Winsley Street			185	**McDonald's** Restaurant
			187	**Bankrupt Clothing Co** Fashion FM
Fashion M **Blazer**	170		189	**Next** Fashion FM
Sportswear **Cobra**	172			
Fashion F **Richards**	174			
Baby store **Mothercare**	174			
Fashion FM **Mark-One**	178			
Great Titchfield Street				**Ramilles Street**
			199	**Leslie Davis** Jewellers
Shoes FM **Ravel**	184		201	**Paperchase** Gifts
Sock Shop	190		213	**LITTLEWOODS** STORE
Shoes FM **Faith**	192		217	**Wallis** Fashion F
Midland Bank	196		219	**Knickerbox** Underwear
STORE **C&A**	202			

Left side	No.	No.	Right side
Great Portland Street			*Hills Place*
Restaurant **Burger King**	214	221	**Miss Selfridge** Fashion F
Fashion F **Anne Brooks** (Petite Fashion)	216	225	**Benetton** Fashion FM
Fashion F **Evans**	218	227	**Crest of London** Souvenirs
		229	**Strings Sale Depot** Fashion FM
		231	**Jeans West** Fashion FM
		233	**The Byrite Company** Fashion M
		235	Thomas Cook Bureau de change
			Argyll Street
STORE **TOP SHOP & TOP MAN**	214-216	241	Exchange International Bureau de change
		266	**Shellys** Shoes FM
Oxford Circus	⊖		*Regent Street*
Fashion F **Hennes**	238	251	South African Airways
		257	**Sock Shop**
John Prince's Street		261	For Eyes Opticians
		263	**Richards** Fashion F
Fashion M **Mister Byrite**	244	267	**J. D. Sports** Sportswear
Shoes FM **Bally**	246	271	**La Baguette Parisienne** Take-away food
Shoes FM **Ravel**	248	273	**Scottish Woollens** Fashion, knitwear
Jewellers **H. Samuel**	250	275	Salvation Army Hall
STORE **BHS**	252	277	**Ernest Jones** Jewellers
Shoes FM **Clarks**	260	283	**River Island** Fashion FM
Fashion F **Jane Norman**	262	285	**Boots** Chemist
Fashion F **Monsoon**	264	287	**Cecil Gee** Fashion M
Fashion F **Ann Harvey**	266	289	**The Deep Pan Pizza Co** Restaurant
Natural beauty products **The Body Shop**	268	291	Bureau de change
Greetings cards **Clinton**	270	291	**Mr Howard** Fashion M
Fashion F **Wallis**	272	291	**Shirts, Ties & Sock Shop** Fashion FM
		291b	**McDonald's** Restaurant
Holles Street			*Harewood Place*
		293	**Accessorize** Accessories
STORE **JOHN LEWIS**	273-306	295	**Tie Rack** Fashion FM
		297	**Saxone** Shoes FM
		299	**Babers** Shoes M
		299	Noel Nursing agency
		301	**Olympus Sports** Sports goods and sportswear
Old Cavendish Street		303	**Tesco Metro** Foodstore
		309	**Swatch** Watches
STORE **D.H. EVANS**	318	315	Acme Employment agency
		315	**The Gap** Fashion FM, childrenswear
Chapel Place			*Dering Street*
Shoes FM **K Shoes**	324	321	**Stefanel** Fashion FM
Sock Shop	326	321	Berlitz School of Languages
Fashion FM **Naf Naf**	328	321	**Next** Fashion M
Smokers' materials **Bond's**	328	325	**Next** Fashion F
Bank of Scotland	332		
Vere Street			*New Bond Street*
STORE **DEBENHAMS**	344-348	333	**Dolcis** Shoes FM
		335	**Splash** Souvenirs
		337	**Bonjour Paris** Take-away food
		339	Bureau de change
		347	**Café Zeynah** Take-away food
		341	**Wendy's** Restaurant
Marylebone Lane			*Woodstock Street*
Ties, shirts **Off The Cuff**	350	351	**Le Croissant** Take-away food
Telephones **British Telecom Shop**	350	353	**Thorntons** Chocolates
TSB Bank	350	353	Brook Street Employment agency
		355	**House of Cashmere** Fashion FM
Marylebone Lane		357	**Selection** Fashion FM
Souvenirs **Crest of London**	354		*Sedley Place*
Fashion FM **Tie Rack**	356		
Accessories **Sunglass Hut**	357	359	**Churchill** Gifts
National Westminster Bank	358	361	**Oakland** Fashion M
		363	**HMV Shop** Records, CDs & cassettes
		369	**La Brioche Dorée** Take-away food
		369a	Foreign Exchange Corporation
		⊖	Bond Street
		373	**Leslie Davis** Jewellers
Stratford Place			*Davies Street (South Molton Street)*
Shoes FM **Lilley & Skinner**	360	379	**Burtons/Dorothy Perkins** Fashion FM
Fashion F **Kookai**	362	379	**WEST ONE SHOPPING CENTRE**
Fashion M **Woodhouse**	364	383	**Faith** Shoes F
Jewellers **H. Samuel**	366	385	**Boots** Chemist
		393	**Jeans West** Fashion FM
St Christopher's Place		395	**The Gap** Fashion FM
Shoes FM **Bally**	368		
Fashion M **Suits You**	370		
Natural beauty products **The Body Shop**	372		
James Street			*Gilbert Street*
STORE **C&A**	376	399	**Pizzaland** Restaurant
		399	Lloyds Bank
Bird Street			*Binney Street*
Shoes FM **Instep Sports**	386	407	**Eisenegger** Fashion M
Fashion F **Jane Norman**	388	409	**Bertie** Shoes FM
Shoes FM **Barratts**	388	409	**Bruce Jeremy** Fashion M
		411	Kelly Temporary services Employment agency
		413	**Mappin & Webb** Jewellers

Left side	No.	No.	Right side
Duke Street			**Duke Street**
		415	**Ciro Citterio** *Fashion M*
		419	**Principles** *Fashion FM*
			Lumley Street
		425	**Review** *Fashion M*
		427	**Samuel Maynard** *China & gifts*
		429	**Burger King** *Restaurant*
STORE **SELFRIDGES**	400		
			Balderton Street
		431	Midland Bank
		435	**Sock Shop**
		439	**Boots** *Chemist*
		443	British Nursing Association
		443	**Churchill** *Gifts*
		445	**London House** *Fashion FM*
		447	**Grip** *Fashion M*
		449	**Jean Jeanie** *Fashion FM*
		451	**Laura Ashley** *Fashion F*
Orchard Street			**North Audley Street**
STORE **MARKS & SPENCER**	458	455	**American Burger** *Restaurant*
National Westminster Bank	466	461	**Mothercare** *Baby store*
Shoes FM **Bally**	468	467	**House of Scotland** *Fashion FM*
Jewellers **H. Samuel**	472	469	**Knickerbox** *Underwear*
Shoes FM **Clarks**	476	471	**House of Cashmere** *Cashmeres*
Fashion F **Etam**	484	473	**Jacadi** *Childrenswear*
Chemist **Boots**	488	473	**Adams** *Childrenswear*
Shoes FM **Russell & Bromley**	494	479	**Aberdeen Steak House** *Restaurant*
Travel goods **Baggage Company**	498	481	**Hennes** *Fashion F*
Watches of Switzerland	500	483	**Oakland** *Fashion F*
Shoes FM **Saxone**	502	485	**The Highlands** *Fashion FM*
		487	Alfred Marks *Employment agency*
		487	**Tie Rack** *Fashion FM*
		489	**Boy Trading Co** *Fashion M*
		491	**Ryman** *Stationery*
		493	**Dixons** *Cameras & electronics*
STORE **LITTLEWOODS**	506		**Park Street**
Fashion FM **Benetton**	522	505	**C&A** *STORE*
Novelty goods **Cascade**	524	523	**Pizza Hut** *Restaurant*
Fashion F **Next**	526	527	**Virgin Records** *Records, CDs & cassettes*
Travel goods **Salisburys**	530	537	**Cerex** *Souvenirs*
Fashion F **Wallis**	532		
Fashion F **Evans**	538		
Old Quebec Street			
Restaurant **Kentucky Fried Chicken**	542		**Park Lane**
Bureau de change **Chequepoint**	548		
Marble Arch	⊖		
Bureau de change **Berkeley Credit**	550		
Cumberland Hotel	552		
China & glass **Chinacraft**	556		
Great Cumberland Place			**Marble Arch**

Bond Street – new and old

Left side	No.	No.	Right side
Oxford Street			**Oxford Street**
Shoes FM **Dolcis**	87	325	**Next** *Fashion F*
Fashion F **Warehouse**	89	81	**Berkertex Brides** *Bridalwear*
Fashion M **Blazer**	90		
Fashion M **Cecil Gee**	92		
Fashion FM **Pringle of Scotland**	92		
Restaurant **Mirinae**	94		
Shoes FM **Grant**	94		
Blenheim Street			**Dering Street**
Shoes F **Carvela**	95		
Royal Bank of Scotland	97		
Linens **Frette**	98	75	**Cerruti 1881** *Fashion M*
Employment agency Manpower	98	74	**Alexander Juran** *Oriental carpets*
Fashion F **Betty Barclay**	99	74	**Paul Kaye** *Portrait photographer*
Shoes FM **Lanzoni**	100	73	**Louis Feraud** *Fashion F*
Auctioneers **Phillips**	101	72	**Timberland** *Fashion M*
Jewellers **Watches of Bond Street**	102	70	**Susan Woolf** *Fashion F*
Leather goods **Henry's**	103	70	**Kabaret** *Bar*
Shoes F **Ivory**	104	69	**Please Mum** *Childrenswear*
Fashion F **Laurel**	105	68	**Robina** *Fashion F*
Fashion F **Cerruti**	105-6	66	**Escada** *Fashion F*
Fashion F **Alexon**	107	65	**Guy Laroche** *Fashion F*
Fashion F **Lanvin**	108	64	**Dixons** *Cameras & electronics*
Sylvia Lewis Beauty Clinic	108		
Hairdressing salon **Stephen Way Hair**	109		
Shoes FM **Russell & Bromley**	109		

Brook Street			**Brook Street**
Bond Street Silver Galleries	111	63	**FENWICK** STORE
Shoes FM **Bally**	116		
Fashion M **Cecil Gee**	120		
Lane Fine Art	123		
Arcade **Bond Street Antiques Centre**	124	54	**Louis Vuitton** Fashion F
Fashion M **Herbie Frogg**	125	53	**Jasons** Fabrics
Photography **Wallace Heaton**	126	51	**The White House** Linen
Midland Bank	129	50	**Chappell Music Centre**
		49	**Bruno Magli** Shoes FM
		47	**F. Pinet** Shoes FM

Grosvenor Street			**Maddox Street**
Fashion F, leather goods **Loewe**	130	46	**Avi Rossini** Fashion M
Fashion FM **Beale & Inman**	131	46	**Ciao** Travel
Shoes FM **Church's Shoes**	133	45	**Massada** Antiques
Fabrics **Simmonds**	134	43	**Smythson** Leather goods
Fashion M **Yves Saint Laurent**	135	41	**Herbie** Fashion M
Fashion F **Yves Saint Laurent**	137	40	**Vittorio Arzani** Fashion M
		38	**Riyahi Gallery** Fine art

Bloomfield Place			38	**Pal Zileri** Fashion M
			37	**Ermenegildo Zegna** Fashion FM
Fashion F **Marie Claire**	138	36	**Fogal** Lace
Silver & goldsmiths **S. J. Phillips**	139	34	**Sotheby's** Auctioneers
Fashion FM **Zilli**	140	32	**Richard Green** Paintings
Antiques **Mallett**	141	31	**Fior** Jewellers
Fashion FM **Polo Ralph Lauren**	143	30	**Herbert Johnson** Milliner FM
Antiques **Frank Partridge**	144	29	**Gordon Scott** Shoes FM
Fine art dealers **Wildenstein**	147	28	**Celine** Accessories F
Fine Art Society	148	27	**Wana Designs** Fashion FM
Luggage **Louis Vuitton**	149	26	**Tessiers** Gold & silversmiths
		24	**Russell & Bromley** Shoes FM

Bruton Street			**Conduit Street**
Publishers **Time & Life**	155	23a	**Philip Landau** Fashion M
Luxury goods **Hermes**	155	23	**Moira** Antiques
Cashmeres **Ballantyne**	153a	22	**Moira** Antiques
Fashion F **Max Mara**	157	22	**European Suit Store** Fashion M
Fashion FM **Valentino**	160	19	**Tecno** Modern furniture
Paintings **John Mitchell & Son**	160	18	**Krizia** Fashion F
Glass **Lalique**	162	17	Air India
Shoes M **Church's Shoes**	163		
Employment agency **Kelly Temporary Services**	163		
Fashion FM **Savoy Tailors Guild**	164		

			Clifford Street
		16	**Watches of Switzerland**

Grafton Street			15	**Patek Phillipe** Watches
Luxury accessories **Asprey**	165	15	**Georg Jensen** Silversmiths
Jewellers **Collingwood**	171	14a	**Chopard** Luxury goods
Jewellers **Bulgari**	172	14a	**Adler of Geneva** Jewellers
Fashion F **Karl Lagerfeld**	173	12	**Hennell** Silversmiths
Gallery **Lalaounis**	174	11	**Philip Antrobus** Jewellers
Jewellers **Cartier**	175	10	**Adele Davis** Fashion F
Shoes & leatherwear **Rossetti**	177	10a	**Anne Bloom** Jewellers
Fashion FM **Henry Cotton's**	179	9	**Ciro** Jewellers
Jewellers **Tiffany & Co**	25	8	**Bentley & Co** Antiques
Fashion F **Chanel**	26	7	**Graff** Jewellers
The Royal Arcade	28	4	**Richard Green** Art gallery
Silver & jewellery **Holmes**	29	1	National Westminster Bank
Historical Portraits Ltd	30		
Shoes FM **Bally**	30		**Burlington Gardens**
Luxury goods **Gucci**	33		
		24	**Salvatore Ferragamo** Shoes FM & accessories
		22	**Chatila** Jewellers
		19	**A. Sulka & Co** Fashion M
		17	**Rashid** Carpets
Stafford Street		17	**Clough** Jewellers & pawnbrokers
Fashion FM **Gianni Versace**	36	17	**Tom Gilbey Waistcoat Gallery** Fashion FM
Fine art **Entwistle**	37	16	**Frost & Reed** Paintings
Antiques **Deborah Gage**	38	15	**Ricci Burns** Fashion F
Marlborough Fine Art Gallery	39	14	**Colnaghi Galleries** Paintings
Lloyds Bank	39	13	**Leger Galleries** Paintings
Employment agency **Success After Sixty**	40	13	**Benson & Hedges** Tobacconist
Fine art **Noortman**	41	10	Lufthansa German Airlines
Fine art **Thos. Agnew & Sons**	43	9	**Ginza Yamagataya** Fashion M
Fine art **Thomas Gibson**	44	7	Air Nippon Airlines
		5	**W. R. Harvey** Antiques
		2	**Kings of Sheffield** Antique silver
		1a	**F. B. Meyrowitz** Opticians
		1	**Watches of Switzerland**

Green Park ⊖			Piccadilly

South Molton Street

Oxford Street

Left side			Right side	
Pub **Hog in the Pound Tavern**	28		35	**Foto Inn** *Developing & printing*
Employment agency **Select Appointments**	28		36	**Bertie** *Shoes FM*
Designer fashion F **Browns**	23		37	**Leather Rat** *Leather fashion FM*
Teas & Coffees **Whittards**	22		39	**Gigli** *Fashion FM*
Bond Street Secretarial Bureau	22		40	**The Red Rock Café**
Japanese jewellery **Electrum**	21		41	**The Tube** *Shoes & fashion F*
Fashion jewellery **Butler & Wilson**	20		42	**Alma** *Fashion M*
Shoes FM **Pied à Terre**	19		43	**Saga** *Japanese restaurant*
Fashion F **Genny**	18		45	**Hexagone** *Fashion F*
Employment agency **Reed**	17		45	ROC Recruitment *Secretarial agency*
Fashion M **Joseph**	16		45	**Karen Millen** *Fashion F*
Fashion F **Stefanel**	15		46	**Widow Applebaum's** *Jewish restaurant*
Fashion F **French for Less**	14		47	**Hobbs** *Fashion & shoes F*
Shoes FM **Rider**	13		48	**Grosvenor Gallery**
Designer fashion F **Arte**	12		48	**Cable & Co** *Fashion M*
Restaurant **Grand Café**	11		49	**Skindeep** *Leather fashions FM*
Fashion F **Pied a Terre**	9		50	**Browns Labels for Less** *Fashion FM*
Hats **The Hat Shop**	8		51	**Vertice** *Italian fashion FM*
Fashion FM **Sisley**	6		52	**Anvers** *Fashion FM*
Designer jewellery **André Bogaert**	5		53	**Geno Ventti** *Hairdressing salon*
Designer jewellery **Agatha**	4		54	**Fabrice Karel** *Fashion F*
Handbags & luggage **City Bag Store**	3		54	Reed Accountancy *Employment agency*
Fashion M **Daniel James**	2		55	**Oliver** *Fashion M*
Shoes FM **Podium**	1		56	**Bang & Olufson** *TV & hi-fi*
Restaurant **Wheelers**	1			
Fashion F **Ronit Zilkha**	34			

Globe Yard

			Right side	
			57	**Adolfo Dominguez** *Hairdressing salon*
			57	**Molton Brown** *Hairdressing salon*
			59	Shane English School
			60	**Office** *Shoes FM*
			60	**Vidal Sassoon** *Hairdressing salon*
			64	**South Molton Drug Stores**
			65	Post Office
			66	**Kenneth Jay Lane** *Jewellers*
			67	**Monsoon** *Fashion F*
			68	**Celia Loe** *Fashion F*

Regent Street

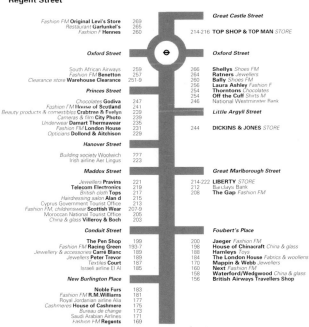

Great Castle Street

Left side			Right side	
Fashion FM **Original Levi's Store**	269			
Restaurant **Garfunkel's**	265			
Fashion F **Hennes**	260		214-216	**TOP SHOP & TOP MAN** *STORE*

Oxford Street | | | **Oxford Street**

Left side			Right side	
South African Airways	259		266	**Shellys** *Shoes FM*
Fashion FM **Benetton**	257		264	**Ratners** *Jewellers*
Clearance store **Warehouse Clearance**	251-9		260	**Bally** *Shoes FM*
			256	**Laura Ashley** *Fashion F*
Princes Street			254	**Thorntons** *Chocolates*
			254	**Off the Cuff** *Shirts M*
Chocolates **Godiva**	247		246	National Westminster Bank
Fashion FM **House of Scotland**	241			
Beauty products & comestibles **Crabtree & Evelyn**	239			**Little Argyll Street**
Cameras & film **City Photo**	239			
Underwear **Damart Thermawear**	235		244	**DICKINS & JONES** *STORE*
Fashion FM **London House**	231			
Opticians **Dollond & Aitchison**	229			

Hanover Street

Left side			Right side	
Building society **Woolwich**	???			
Irish airline **Aer Lingus**	223			

Maddox Street | | | **Great Marlborough Street**

Left side			Right side	
Jewellers **Pravins**	221		214-222	**LIBERTY** *STORE*
Telecom **Electronics**	219		212	Barclays Bank
British cloth **Tops**	217		208	**The Gap** *Fashion M*
Hairdressing salon **Alan d**	215			
Cyprus Government Tourist Office	213			
Fashion FM, childrenswear **Scottish Wear**	207-9			
Moroccan National Tourist Office	205			
China & glass **Villeroy & Boch**	203			

Conduit Street | | | **Foubert's Place**

Left side			Right side	
The Pen Shop	199		200	**Jaeger** *Fashion FM*
Fashion FM **Racing Green**	193-7		198	**House of Chinacraft** *China & glass*
Jewellery & accessories **Carré Blanc**	189		188	**Hamleys** *Toys*
Jewellers **Peter Trevor**	189		184	**The London House** *Fabrics & woollens*
Textiles **Court**	187		170	**Mappin & Webb** *Jewellers*
Israeli airline **El Al**	185		160	**Next** *Fashion FM*
			158	**Waterford/Wedgwood** *China & glass*
New Burlington Place			156	**British Airways Travellers Shop**

Left side		
Noble Furs	183	
Fashion FM **R.M. Williams**	181	
Royal Jordanian airline **Alia**	177	
Cashmeres **House of Cashmere**	175	
Bureau de change	173	
Saudi Arabian Airlines	171	
Fashion FM **Regents**	169	

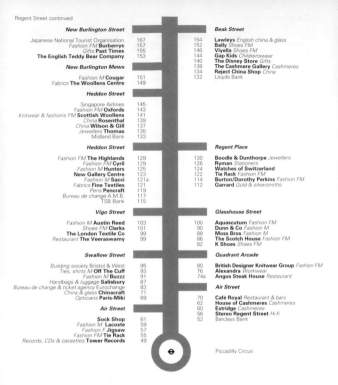

New Burlington Street

			Beak Street
Japanese National Tourist Organisation	167	154	**Lawleys** English china & glass
Fashion FM **Burberrys**	157	152	**Bally** Shoes FM
Gifts **Past Times**	155	146	**Viyella** Shoes FM
The English Teddy Bear Company	153	144	**Gap Kids** Childrenswear
		140	**The Disney Store** Gifts
New Burlington Mews		138	**The Cashmere Gallery** Cashmeres
		134	**Reject China Shop** China
Fashion M **Cougar**	151	132	Lloyds Bank
Fabrics **The Woollens Centre**	149		

Heddon Street

Singapore Airlines	145
Fashion FM **Oxfords**	143
Knitwear & fashions FM **Scottish Woollens**	141
China **Rosenthal**	139
China **Wilson & Gill**	137
Jewellers **Thomas**	135
Midland Bank	133

Heddon Street

			Regent Place
Fashion FM **The Highlands**	129	130	**Boodle & Dunthorpe** Jewellers
Fashion FM **Cyril**	129	126	**Ryman** Stationers
Fashion FM **Hunters**	125	124	**Watches of Switzerland**
New Gallery Centre	123	122	**Tie Rack** Fashion FM
Fashion M **Sacci**	121a	114	**Burton/Dorothy Perkins** Fashion FM
Fabrics **Fine Textiles**	121	112	**Garrard** Gold & silversmiths
Pens **Pencraft**	119		
Bureau de change A.M.B.	117		
TSB Bank	115		

Vigo Street

			Glasshouse Street
Fashion M **Austin Reed**	103	100	**Aquascutum** Fashion FM
Shoes FM **Clarks**	101	90	**Dunn & Co** Fashion M
The London Textile Co	99	88	**Moss Bros** Fashion M
Restaurant **The Veeraswamy**	99	86	**The Scotch House** Fashion FM
		82	**K Shoes** Shoes FM

Swallow Street

			Quadrant Arcade
Building society Bristol & West	95	80	**British Designer Knitwear Group** Fashion FM
Ties, shirts M **Off The Cuff**	93	76	**Alexandra** Workwear
Fashion M **Buzzz**	91	74a	**Angus Steak House** Restaurant
Handbags & luggage **Salisbury**	87		
Bureau de change & ticket agency Eurochange	83		**Air Street**
China & glass **Chinacraft**	71		
Opticians **Paris-Miki**	69	70	**Café Royal** Restaurant & bars
		62	**House of Cashmeres** Cashmeres
Air Street		60	**Estridge** Cashmeres
		56	**Stereo Regent Street** Hi-fi
Sock Shop	61	52	Barclays Bank
Fashion M **Lacoste**	59		
Fashion F **Jigsaw**	57		
Fashion FM **Tie Rack**	55		
Records, CDs & cassettes **Tower Records**	49		

Piccadilly Circus

Kings Road

Sloane Square

			Sloane Square
STORE **PETER JONES**			Sloane Square
		9	Post Office
		11	**The Coffee Shop**
		11	**HoHo** Chinese restaurant
		13	**Naf Naf** Fashion FM
		15	**Osh Kosh B'gosh** Childrenswear
		17	**Roberto's** Nightclub
		21	Ladbrokes Bookmakers
		23	**Forbuoys** Newsagents & tobacconists
		25	**Lazer** Fashion M
		27	Eurochange Bureau de change
		31	**Astuces** Fashion F
			Duke of York's Headquarters

Cadogan Gardens

Childrenswear & accessories **Trotters**	34
Children's playthings **Early Learning Centre**	36
Fashion F **Hampstead Bazaar**	38
Fashion F **Sidney Smith**	36
London School of Bridge	38
Fashion M **Cecil Gee**	44
Wine Bar **Blushes**	52
Natural beauty products **The Body Shop**	54
Fashion FM **Jeans West**	54
Restaurant **Pizza Hut**	56
Chemist **Boots**	58
Shoes FM **Russell & Bromley**	64
Sock Shop	68

Blacklands Terrace

Fashion FM, childrenswear, home furnishings **Next**	72

Lincoln Street

Boulangerie/pâtisserie **Guys & Dolls**	74
Fashion F **Oasis**	76
Restaurant **Pizzaland**	80
Fashion FM **Esprit**	82
Shoes FM **Hobbs**	84
Fashion F **Jeffrey Rogers**	86
Fashion FM **Stefanel**	88
Shoes FM **Cable & Co**	90
Shoes FM **Bally**	92
Fashion F **Benetton**	94
Fashion F **Warehouse**	96
Restaurant **The Chelsea Kitchen**	98
Shoes FM **Office London**	100
Fashion F **Stirling Cooper**	102
Fashion F **Longpoint Bay**	104
Fashion FM **Petroleum**	106

Anderson Street

Building Society **Chelsea**	112
Fashion M **Reiss**	114

Tryon Street

Fashion FM **The Leather Warehouse**	118
Shoes FM **Bertie**	118
Fashion F **Laura Ashley**	120
Fashion FM & childrenswear **Gap**	122
SHOPPING MALL KINGS WALK	
Fashion F **Kookai**	124
Fashion M **Woodhouse**	124a
Shoes FM **Shellys**	124b
Fashion F **Jigsaw**	124c
Fashion F **Et Vous**	126
Shoes FM **Ravel**	128
Bureau de change **Chequepoint**	130
Fashion F **Moa**	132

Bywater Street

Beauty products & comestibles **Crabtree & Evelyn**	134
Fashion FM **Legacy**	136
Building society **Abbey National**	138
Ice-cream **Haagen-Dazs**	138a

Markham Square

Fashion FM **French Connection**	140
Greetings cards **Post Impressions**	146

Markham Street

Chemist **Boots**	150
Restaurant **The Pheasantry**	152
Stationery **Ryman**	152
Books **Dillons**	152

Jubilee Place

Lloyds Bank	164
Fashion FM **Chelsea Leather**	168
Film processing **Snappy Snaps**	170
Restaurant **Choy's**	172
Shoes FM **Blue Velvet**	174
Opticians **Chelsea Eye Centre**	176

Burnsall Street

Fashion F **Blu di Blu**	178
Shoes FM **R. Soles**	178a
Fashion FM **Forest Ranger**	182
New age gifts **Paradise Farm**	182a
Teas & coffees **Whittard**	184
Fashion FM **Soldier Blue**	184a

Cheltenham Terrace

33	National Westminster Bank
33a	**Blazer** Fashion M
33b	**Dune** Shoes FM
33c	**Chipie** Fashion M
33d	**Monsoon** Fashion F
33e	**Martins of Chelsea** TV & hi-fi
33f	**David Clulow** Opticians
33g	**Pied a Terre** Shoes FM
33h	**Our Price** Records, CDs & cassettes

Walpole Street

35	**Safeway** Supermarket

Royal Avenue

49	**McDonald's** Restaurant
51	**Miso** Designer clearance store
53	**Pineapple** Designer clearance store
55	**Oddbins** Wine merchants
57	**Helen Storey** Fashion F
59	**Karen Millen** Fashion F

Wellington Street

61	**Dentics** Dentist
63	**Renegade** Shoes FM
65	**Sonico Jeans** Fashion FM
67a	**Harvest** Leather fashion M
69	**Designerwear Clearance Sale** Designer clearance sto

Smith Street

69a	**Sissors** Hairdressing salon
71	**Morgan** Fashion F
73	**Bruce Jeramy** Fashion F
75	**In Wear** Fashion FM
77	**Benihana** Restaurant
79	**New Man** Fashion M
85	**MARKS & SPENCER** STORE
95	**The Pier** Household goods & furnishings
97	**Cotton Club** Fashion F
99	**Woodhouse** Fashion M
	Car Park
1Ub	**Ware on Earth** Household goods
107	**Liaison** Nightclub
109a	**R. Soles** Leather boots
109	**The Poster Shop**
113	**Rivaaz** Leatherwear FM
115	**Kodo** Fashion F

Radnor Walk

119	**Chelsea Potter** Pub
121	**The Common Market** Fashion FM
123	**Victoria Wine** Wine merchants
123a	**Awards** Fashion FM

Shawfield Street

125	**Wax Lyrical** Candles
127	**Picasso** Restaurant
129	**Juke Box** Fashion M
131	**Gore Booker** Interior goods
135	**Antiquarius** Antiques, clothes
137	**Basia Zarsycka** Bridalwear, shoes, jewellery
139	**Quincy** Fashion M
141	**Edwina Ronay** Fashion F

Flood Street

Left side	No.		No.	Right side
Dry cleaners **Sketchley**	186		145	**Jaeger** Fashion FM
Leather fashion FM **Sloane's Leathers**	186a		147	**Quarzo** Fashion FM
Clearance store **The Designer Outlet**	188a		150	**Omcar** Fashion FM
Natural goods **Natural Fact**	192		151	**Shoe Repairs & Things** Shoe repair
Candles **Angelic**	196		153	**Boy** Fashion M
Supermarket **Waitrose**	198		155	**Original Levi's Store** Fashion
Pub **The Trafalgar**	200		155a	Chelsea Methodist Church
Chelsea Cinema	206		157	**Hittite** Fashion F
Furnishings **Habitat**	206		159	**Skindeep** Leather fashion FM
			161	**The Boot Store** Shoes M

Chelsea Manor Street — **Chelsea Manor Street**

Left side	No.		No.	Right side
National Westminster Bank	224			TOWN HALL
Post Office	232			Citizen's Advice Bureau
Household goods **Reject Shop**	234		181	**Chenil Galleries** Antiques
			183	**The Garage** Designer fashion FM
			185	**David Clulow** Opticians
Sydney Street			187	**Photo-Optix** Cameras
			191	**Phlip** Fashion FM
COUNCIL OFFICES	250		193	**Steinberg & Tolkien** Antique clothing & jewellery
			195	**Henry J Bean's Bar & Grill** Bar
			199	**Prime Video** Videos
Dovehouse Street			201	**Amagansett** Fashion M
			203	**Chelsea Audio-Visual Centre**
			205	**Pucci Pizza** Italian restaurant
CHELSEA FIRE STATION			207	**Givans** Linen
			209	**Oddbins** Wine merchants

Manresa Road — **Oakley Street**

KING'S COLLEGE LONDON — **Glebe Place**

No.	Right side
219	**David Pettifer** Antiques
221	**My Old Dutch** Restaurant
237	**Chelsea Food Fayre**

Bramerton Street

Left side		No.	Right side
Carlyle Square		241	**Designers Sale Studio** Fashion F
		243	**Ironworks** Ironware
		245	**Nottinghill Housing Trust** Charity shop
		245a	**Chelsea Antique Market**
		247	**Joanna Booth** Antiques
		249	**Made In Italy** Restaurant
		251	**S. Borris** Delicatessen
		253	**Chelsea Antique Market**
		255	**Isaac. T. Lloyd** Chemist
		257	Newsagents
		259	**Green & Stone** Artists' materials
		263	**Ellessential** Hairdressing salon
		265	**Holme Place** Launderers & drycleaners
		271	**Designers Guild** Furnishings
		271b	**The Stockpot** Restaurant
Estate agents De Groot Collis	296	275	**David Tron** Antiques
Pub **Cadogan Arms**	298	277	**Designers Guild** Fabric & wallpapers

Church Street — **Old Church Street**

Left side	No.		No.	Right side
National Westminster Bank	300		279	MGM Cinema
Interior designers **Osborne & Little**	304		279	**Mr Light** Lighting
Antiques **Godson & Coles**	310		279	**Europa Foods** Supermarket
Restaurant **Le Gourmet**	312		279c	**Delcor** Interiors
Artists' materials **Chelsea Art Stores**	314		281	**Brats** Gifts & cards
Restaurant **The Argyll**	316		283	**Wilde One's** Ethnic fashion & gifts
Maps & prints **Old Church Galleries**	320		285	**Shoefax** Shoes FM
Furniture **Shaker**	322		287	**Raffles** Club
Furniture **Sofa Workshop**	324		289	**Sasha Hetherington** Evening wear F
Carpets **Bernadout**	328		289a	**The Jam** Restaurant
Restaurant **Lo Spuntino**	330		289	**Joanna's Tent** Fashion FM & childrenswear
Restaurant **Big Easy**	334			
Antiques **Monro Heywood**	336			
Furniture **William Yeoward**	336			**Paultons Square**
Restaurant **Travellers**	338			
Restaurant **Thierry's**	342			
Antiques **Tony Bunzl**	344		303	**Solino Leather** Leatherwear FM
Barclays Bank	348		305	**Bamboo Kitchen** Chinese take-away
			307	**Chrysalis** Persian & Eastern rugs
The Vale			309	**Million Dollar Sports** Sportswear
			313	**Kaffee Opera** Coffee shop
			317	**Gregor Schumi** Hairdressing salon
Fashion M **The Bad Apple**	350		319	**J. & F. E. Simpson** Jewellers
Fashion M **Nigel Hall**	350		321	**Rococo** Chocolates
Designer fashion FM **The Bluebird Garage**	350		323	**Dept.** Shoes & fashion M
Wellworth Food & Wines	350b			
Fashion M **Daniel James**	352			
National Westminster Bank	352a			**Beaufort Street**

Conversion charts

Clothing Sizes

In London you will find English, Continental and American sizing in clothes shops, whereas there is a combination of English and Continental sizing for shoes.

Dresses

English	10	12	14	16	18	20	22
	32	**34**	**36**	**38**	**40**	**42**	**44**
USA	8	10	12	14	16	18	20
Continental	38	40	42	44	46	48	50

Shoes

English	**3**	**$3\frac{1}{2}$**	**4**	**$4\frac{1}{2}$**	**5**	**$5\frac{1}{2}$**	**6**	**$6\frac{1}{2}$**	**7**	**$7\frac{1}{2}$**	**8**
USA	$4\frac{1}{2}$	5	$5\frac{1}{2}$	6	$6\frac{1}{2}$	7	$7\frac{1}{2}$	8	$8\frac{1}{2}$	9	$9\frac{1}{2}$
Continental	35	36	37	37	38	38	39	40	40	41	41

Hats

English	**$6\frac{5}{8}$**	**$6\frac{3}{4}$**	**$6\frac{7}{8}$**	**7**	**$7\frac{1}{8}$**	**$7\frac{1}{4}$**	**$7\frac{3}{8}$**	**$7\frac{1}{2}$**	**$7\frac{5}{8}$**
USA	$6\frac{3}{4}$	$6\frac{7}{8}$	7	$7\frac{1}{8}$	$7\frac{3}{8}$	$7\frac{1}{2}$			
Continental	54	55	56	57	58	59	60	61	62

Glove sizes are international.

Weights and Measures

Feet/Metres

English	**1**	**2**	**3**	**4**	**5**	**6**	**7**	**8**	**9**	**10**
Continental	0.3	0.6	0.9	1.2	1.5	1.8	2.1	2.4	2.7	3.0

Pounds/Kilograms

English	**1**	**2**	**3**	**4**	**5**	**6**	**7**	**8**	**9**	**10**
Continental	0.4	0.9	1.4	1.8	2.3	2.7	3.2	3.6	4.1	4.5

Pints/Litres

English	**$\frac{1}{4}$**	**$\frac{1}{2}$**	**$\frac{3}{4}$**	**1**	**2**	**3**	**4**	**5**
Continental	0.1	0.3	0.4	0.6	1.1	1.7	2.3	2.8

EATING & DRINKING

Restaurants

These have been chosen for authentic food and good cooking. For more detailed information on where and what to eat see Nicholson's London Restaurant Guide.
Restaurant Services (0181-888 8080) and Direct Dining (0171-287 3287) offer free up-to-the-minute information and advice on London's restaurants and can make table reservations.

The following price guide refers to a three-course meal for one without wine but including VAT:

£ - £10.00 and under
££ - £10.00-£20.00
£££ - £20.00-£30.00
£££+ - £30.00 and over

(Reserve) - advisable to reserve
Open to . . . - last orders

A - Access/Mastercard/Eurocard
Ax - American Express
Dc - Diners Club
V - Visa/Barclaycard

B - breakfast
L - lunch
D - dinner

Service charge: *many restaurants add service on to the bill, usually at 12½%, but do not always say so – if in doubt, ask. However, they do usually say if service is not included.*

AFRICAN & CARIBBEAN
Afric-Carib
1 Stroud Green Rd N4. 0171-263 5464. Restaurant and take-away specialising in spicy Nigerian dishes. Chicken, beef or fish with plantains and yams. Relaxed, informal atmosphere. *LD open to 23.30.* A.V. **£**

Eutens   4 F2
4 Neal's Yard, off Neal St WC2. 0171-240 2769. Large, bright restaurant offering Black British cuisine. Chilli prawns with pimento sauce, pan-fried sea bream, chicken in coconut and coriander. *LD open to 24.00. Closed Sun.* A.V. **££**

AMERICAN

Chicago Rib Shack   3 G5
1 Raphael St SW7. 0171-581 5595. Wood-smoked barbecued
meats with salads and trimmings. Cheesecake, mud pie and
ice-cream to follow. *LD open to 23.45, to 22.45 Sun.* A.Ax.V. **££**

Hard Rock Café   4 C5
150 Old Park Lane W1. 0171-629 0382. Ever popular hamburger
joint, just off Hyde Park Corner. Vast room on two levels with
good quality food and non-stop rock. Occasional queues outside. *LD open to 00.15, to 00.45 Sat.* A.Ax.Dc.V. **££**

Joe Allen   4 F3
13 Exeter St WC2. 0171-836 0651. In a converted Covent
Garden warehouse, this London branch follows the pattern of
its New York and Paris counterparts. Menu of steaks, hamburgers, ribs and chilli followed by cheesecake or brownies.
Fashionably crowded, especially after the theatre. Bar. *LD
(Reserve) open to 00.45, to 24.00 Sun.* No credit cards. **££**

Planet Hollywood   4 E3
13 Coventry St W1. 0171-287 1000. The biggest restaurant in
Europe, packed with movie memorabilia. Burgers, ribs, sword-
fish, pizzas, pasta and Mexican dishes. Bar area. *LD (no reservations) open to 01.00.* A.Ax.Dc.V. **££**

BELGIAN

Belgo Noord   1 D1
72 Chalk Farm Rd NW1. 0171-267 0718. Stylish restaurant
which you enter through a tunnel and where the waiters
wear habits. Moules au gratin, wild boar sausages with
stoemp. Belgian beers. *LD open to 23.30, to 22.30 Sun.*
A.Ax.V. **££** Also Belgo Centraal, 50 Earlham St WC2 (**4 E2**).
0171-813 2233.

CENTRAL EUROPEAN

Kerzenstüberl   4 B2
9 St Christopher's Place W1. 0171-486 3196. Authentic
Austrian dishes accompanied by accordion music, dancing and
singing. *LD (Reserve) open to 22.45. Licensed to 01.00.
Closed Sat L & Sun.* A.Ax.Dc.V. **££**

St Moritz   4 E3
161 Wardour St W1. 0171-734 3324. Two floors rigged out
like a ski hut in the famous Swiss resort. Cheese and beef
fondues are the house speciality. *LD (Reserve) open to 23.30.
Closed Sat L & Sun.* A.Ax.Dc.V. **££**

CHINESE

Ken Lo's Memories of China   7 A2
67-69 Ebury St SW1. 0171-730 7734. The windows are etched
with Tang dynasty horses and the menu features regional
specialities: Shanghai sea bass, Szechuan crispy beef,

Cantonese seafood with black bean sauce. *LD open to 23.00, to 22.00 Sun.* A.Ax.Dc.V. **£££**

Lee Ho Fook   4 E3

15-16 Gerrard St W1. 0171-439 1830. Renowned Cantonese cooking, very popular with the local Chinese. Huge portions at reasonable prices. Dim sum at *lunchtime*. *LD open to 23.30, to 24.00 Sat, to 23.00 Sun.* A.Ax.V. **££**

West Zender   4 F3

4a Upper St Martin's Lane WC2. 0171-497 0376. Stylishly designed, you walk over a thick, glass gangplank to enter this restaurant, one of the Zen chain. Modern Oriental menu with a huge choice of noodle dishes. *LD open to 23.30, to 23.00 Sun.* A.Ax.Dc.V. **££**

EAST EUROPEAN
Borshtch 'n' Tears   3 G6

46 Beauchamp Place SW3. 0171-589 5003. Crowded, informal and lively Russian restaurant. Borshtch, beef Stroganoff, chicken Dragomiroff and blinis served to the accompaniment of Russian music. *D open to 01.00, to 00.30 Sun.* Ax. **££**

Daquise   6 D2

20 Thurloe St SW7. 0171-589 6117. Polish restaurant popular with Polish émigrés. Serves traditional, simple and inexpensive dishes: borshtch, bigor and sausages. Also afternoon tea with excellent pastries. *LD open to 23.00.* No credit cards. **£**

Gay Hussar   4 E2

2 Greek St W1. 0171-437 0973. Intimate, cosy, much-loved Hungarian restaurant. Try the stuffed cabbage, chilled wild cherry soup, pike with beetroot sauce. *LD (Reserve) open to 22.45. Closed Sun.* A.Ax.Dc.V. **£££**

ENGLISH
English House   6 F2

3 Milner St SW3. 0171-584 3002. Intimate restaurant in the style of an English country house. Classic English cooking. *LD (Reserve) open to 23.30, to 22.00 Sun.* A.Ax.Dc.V. **£££+**

Rules   4 F3

35 Maiden Lane WC2. 0171-836 5314. Something of a landmark, rich in associations – Dickens, Thackeray, Edward VII and Lillie Langtry all dined here. Jugged hare, steak and kidney pie, grouse and venison. Booking essential. *LD (Reserve) open to 24.00.* A.Ax.V. **£££**

Simpson's-in-the-Strand   4 F3

100 Strand WC2. 0171-836 9112. A British institution with an Edwardian club atmosphere. Excellent fish and meat dishes –

smoked salmon, Dover sole, duck or saddle of mutton. Fine wines and vintage port. Booking and correct dress essential. *LD (Reserve) open to 23.00. Closed Sun.* A.Ax.Dc.V. **£££**

Tiddy Dols   **4 C4**
55 Shepherd Market W1. 0171-499 2357. Unique, comfortable restaurant spreading over several houses dating from 1741. Low ceilings and winding staircases abound. Fillet of venison, beef Wellington, cock-a-leekie and the original gingerbread Tiddy Dol on the menu. Live entertainment. *D (Reserve) open to 23.30.* A.Ax.V. **£££**

FISH
Bentley's   **4 D3**
11-15 Swallow St W1. 0171-734 4756. Famous seafood restaurant and oyster bar. Wide variety of fish, plus excellent oysters, prawns and crab. *LD (Reserve) open to 22.30. Closed Sun.* A.Ax.Dc.V. **£££+**

Café Fish   **4 E3**
39 Panton St SW1. 0171-930 3999. Blackboard menu with a wide and often unusual selection of fish. From raw oysters to battered haddock or trout with shredded vegetables and lemon grass. Good white wines. *LD (Reserve) open to 23.00. Closed Sun.* A.Ax.Dc.V. **££**

Sheekey's   **4 F3**
28 St Martin's Court WC2. 0171-240 2565. One of London's oldest fish restaurants. Excellent oysters, lobster and turbot. Crowded and theatrical. *LD open to 23.15. Closed Sun.* A.Ax.Dc.V. **£££**

Wheeler's Old Compton Street   **4 E2**
19 Old Compton St W1. 0171-437 2706. Popular chain of restaurants specialising in expertly cooked fish dishes. Welcoming yet sophisticated atmosphere. Scallops, lobster, sole and shellfish. Several other branches. *LD (Reserve) open to 23.15, to 22.30 Sun.* A.Ax.Dc.V. **£££**

FRENCH
Auberge de Provence   **4 D6**
St James's Court Hotel, 41 Buckingham Gate SW1. 0171-821 1899. Rustic hotel dining room; provençal inspired cooking. Marinated monkfish, salad of foie gras, lamb with fennel mousse. Provençal wines. *LD (Reserve) open to 23.00. Closed Sat L & Sun.* A.Ax.Dc.V. **£££+**

Chez Nico at Ninety Park Lane   **4 B3**
Grosvenor House Hotel, 90 Park Lane W1. 0171-409 1290. Formal, yet relaxed restaurant serving classic French dishes. *LD (Reserve) open to 23.00. Closed Sat L & Sun LD.* A.Ax.Dc.V. *L* **£££** *D* **£££+**

L'Epicure 4 E2
28 Frith St W1. 0171-437 2829. Confident, flamboyant establishment with excellent French cuisine. Speciality is flambés, also steak maison, crêpes suzette and kidneys in marsala. *LD (Reserve) open to 23.15. Closed Sat L & Sun.* A.Ax.Dc.V. **£££**

L'Escargot 4 E2
48 Greek St W1. 0171-437 6828. A Soho institution. Restaurant on the ground floor offers reasonably priced and varied dishes; upstairs the dining room is more formal. Menu changes every month. Excellent wine list. *LD (Reserve) open to 23.30. Closed Sat L & Sun.* A.Ax.Dc.V. **£££**

Le Gavroche 4 B3
43 Upper Brook St W1. 0171-408 0881. One of the best restaurants in London, renowned for its luxurious atmosphere and imaginative *haute cuisine.* Cooking and service faultless. *LD (Reserve) open to 23.00. Closed Sat & Sun.* A.Ax.Dc.V. **£££**+

GREEK, TURKISH & CYPRIOT
Cypriana 4 D1
11 Rathbone St W1. 0171-636 1057. Traditional Cypriot food in airy surroundings. Specialities are kleftiko, afelia, stifado, dolmades. *LD open to 23.00. Closed Sat L & Sun.* A.Ax.Dc.V. **££**

Lemonia 1 B1
89 Regent's Park Rd NW1. 0171-586 7454. Mediterranean atmosphere in this busy Greek restaurant. Wonderful meze, lamb souvlaki and fish shashlik. *LD open to 23.30. Closed Sat L & Sun D.* A.V. **££**

Mega Kalamaras 3 C3
76 Inverness Mews W2. 0171-727 9122. Also smaller and less expensive **Micro Kalamaras** 66 Inverness Mews W2 (**3 C3**). 0171-727 5082. True taverna atmosphere. Superb national dishes ranging from dolmades to baklava. *D (Reserve) open to 24.00* (Micro *to 23.00). Closed Sun.* Micro is unlicensed. A.Ax.Dc.V. **££**

White Tower 4 E1
1 Percy St W1. 0171-636 8141. Elegant, first class cuisine in London's first Greek restaurant. Lengthy menu and refined atmosphere; moussaka, shashlik and duck with bulghur. *LD (Reserve) open to 22.30. CLOSED Sat L & Sun.* A.Ax.Dc.V. **£££**

INDIAN
Khan's 3 C2
13-15 Westbourne Grove W2. 0171-727 5420. Vast room with oriental arches and palm tree pillars. Cheap, cheerful and noisy with excellent north Indian cuisine. *LD (Reserve D) open to 24.00.* A.Ax.Dc.V. **£**

Red Fort
4 E2

77 Dean St W1. 0171-437 2115. Widely regarded as one of the best Indian restaurants in London. Warm decor, tropical greenery and soft lighting create a palatial atmosphere in which to try Moghul Indian dishes. Quails in mild spice, chicken korahi, tandooris and nan breads. Cocktail bar. *Lunchtime buffet. LD (Reserve) open to 23.00.* A.Ax.Dc.V. **££**

Veeraswamy
4 D3

99-101 Regent St (entrance in Swallow St) W1. 0171-734 1401. Excellent, authentic food in atmosphere of a pre-war Indian club. Traditionally dressed waiters, and a large choice of curries – Moglai, Delhi, Madras, Ceylon and Vindaloo. *LD (Reserve) open to 23.30 Mon-Sat.* A.Ax.Dc.V. **££**

INEXPENSIVE EATING

The following are places where you can eat a good meal for **£10.00 or under**. The café serving 'sausage, egg and chips' is not included here, neither are the fast food chains which can be found on nearly every high street. This list features restaurants with distinctive or unusual cooking and atmosphere – but particularly those that are good value for money.

Chelsea Kitchen
6 E3

98 King's Rd SW3. 0171-589 1330. The daily menu offers a good choice of hot, cheap continental cuisine. Soup, moussaka, spaghetti. Licensed. *LD open to 23.45, to 23.00 Sun.* No credit cards. **£**

Ed's Easy Diner
4 E2

12 Moor St (off Old Compton St) W1. 0171-439 1955. Also at 362 King's Rd SW3 (**6 B6**). 0171-352 1956. American-style diner with counter-top jukeboxes and bar seating. Hamburgers and fries dominate. US beers, thick milkshakes and malts. *LD open to 24.00, to 01.00 Fri & Sat, to 23.00 Sun.* A.V. **£**

Geales
3 B4

2-4 Farmer St W8. 0171-727 7969. Large selection of excellent fish and chips. King prawn rolls, plaice and haddock. Licensed. *LD open to 23.00. Closed Sun & Mon.* A.V. **£**

The Lantern

23a Malvern Rd NW6. 0171-624 1796. Amazing variety and quality at low prices. Simple French bistro with blackboard menu and wine list. Predictably busy. *LD (Reserve Fri & Sat) open to 24.00, to 23.00 Sun.* A.V. **£**

My Old Dutch
4 G1

131 High Holborn WC1. 0171-242 5200. Also at 221 King's Rd SW3 (**6 E4**). 0171-376 5650. Traditional Dutch farmhouse decor, pine tables and chairs. Over 100 generous sized savoury and sweet pancakes. *LD open to 23.45.* A.Ax.Dc.V. **£**

Pollo 4 E2
20 Old Compton St W1. 0171-734 5917. Huge, varied menu at this immensely popular restaurant. Pasta dishes, fish, chicken and steaks. Expect to queue. *LD open to 23.30. Closed Sun.* No credit cards. **£**

Spaghetti House 4 E3
24 Cranbourn St WC2. 0171-836 8168. Genuine Italian spaghetti house, friendly and busy. Soups, pasta dishes, pastries and ice-cream. Several branches. *LD open to 23.00. Closed Sun L.* A.Ax.Dc.V. **£**

Stockpot 4 E3
40 Panton St SW1. 0171-839 5142. Also at 6 Basil St SW3 (**3 G5**). 0171-589 8627. Crowded, noisy and excellent value. Home-made soups, casseroles and puddings. *LD open to 23.15, to 21.45 Sun.* No credit cards. **£**

Wong Kei 4 E3
41-43 Wardour St W1. 0171-437 6833. Large, cheap and cheerful Cantonese restaurant on four floors. Always busy and bustling; expect to share a table! *LD open to 23.30.* No credit cards or cheques. **£**

INTERNATIONAL
Deals West 4 D2
14-16 Foubert's Pl W1. 0171-287 1001. Lively, New-England-style diner decked out in bare wood and brickwork. The menu is American with Thai influences and is divided into 'Raw Deals' – salads, 'Big Deals' – ribs, steaks and burgers, and 'Hot Deals' – Thai curries. *LD open to 23.00, to 02.00 Fri, to 03.00 Sat.* A.Ax.Dc.V. **££**

Pomegranates 7 C4
94 Grosvenor Rd SW1. 0171-828 6560. Highly original and adventurous restaurant. Good value, set price menu is an amalgam of international dishes including Creole, West Indian, Chinese, French and Italian influences. Multi-national wine list. *LD (Reserve D) open to 23.15. Closed Sat L & Sun.* A.Ax.Dc.V. *L* **££** *D* **£££**

Quaglino's 4 D4
16 Bury St SW1. 0171-930 6767. Terence Conran's large and glamorous brasserie seating 400. Varied menu offering crustacea, plateau de fruits de mer, black pudding, roast duck with coriander and ginger. Live music and dancing to *02.00 Fri & Sat. LD (Reserve) open to 24.00, to 01.00 Fri & Sat, to 23.00 Sun.* A.Ax.Dc.V. **£££**

ITALIAN
Biagi's 3 G2
39 Upper Berkeley St W1. 0171-723 0394. Well-run, intimate trattoria decorated with fishing nets. Good varied Italian

dishes. Scallopine alla crema, entrecôte alla pizzaiola, saltimbocca. *LD (Reserve) open to 23.00.* A.Ax.Dc.V. **££**

Kettners   **4 E3**

29 Romilly St W1. 0171-437 6437. There has been a restaurant here since the mid-19thC. Sumptuous interior, probably the most pleasant setting for pizzas and hamburgers. Champagne bar. Pianist *every evening*. *LD (no reservations) open to 24.00.* A.Ax.Dc.V. **££**

Leoni's Quo Vadis   **4 E2**

26-29 Dean St W1. 0171-437 4809. One of Soho's oldest and most famous restaurants, in the same building where Karl Marx once lived. Excellent traditional cuisine; fettucine Quo Vadis, with cream, tomato and fresh basil, is one of the favourites. *LD (Reserve) open to 23.15, to 22.30 Sun.* A.Ax.Dc.V. **£££**

Luigi's   **4 F3**

15 Tavistock St WC2. 0171-240 1795. Something of an institution, often crowded and popular with after-theatre diners. Photographs of entertainment personalities decorate the walls. Good, authentic food: cannelloni, grilled mussels, veal and chicken dishes. *LD (Reserve) open to 23.30. Closed Sun.* A.Dc.V. **£££**

San Lorenzo   **3 G6**

22 Beauchamp Place SW3. 0171-584 1074. One of London's best known Italian restaurants offering excellent traditional cuisine. Fashionable clientele enjoy the unusual veal and chicken dishes. Extensive wine list. Outdoor seating in summer. *LD (Reserve) open to 23.30. Closed Sun.* No credit cards. **£££**

JAPANESE

Masako   **4 B2**

6-8 St Christopher's Place W1. 0171-935 1579. Authentic Japanese restaurant with private dining rooms attended by charming waitresses in kimonos. Wide-ranging menu including set sukiyaki and tempura meals. *LD open to 22.00. Closed Sun.* A.Ax.Dc.V. **£££+**

Wagamama   **4 F1**

4 Streatham St, off Bloomsbury St WC1. 0171-323 9223. Noodle bar with sleek decor. Huge bowls of ramen noodle soup and fried rice or noodles with vegetables or seafood toppings. All served by super-efficient waiters and waitresses wielding hand-held computer pads. Non-smoking. *LD open to 23.00, to 22.00 Sun.* No credit cards. **£**

JEWISH

Bloom's   **5 G2**

90 Whitechapel High St E1. 0171-247 6001. Also at 130 Golders Green Rd NW11. 0181-455 1338. Bustling kosher

restaurants, offering large helpings of gefilte fisch, lockshen pudding, meatballs, salt beef, stuffed kishka. *LD open to 21.30. Closed Fri D, Sat & Jewish hols.* A.Ax.Dc.V. **££**

Widow Applebaum's 4 C3

46 South Molton St W1. 0171-629 4649. American-Jewish deli offering 101 dishes. Matzo balls, hot salt beef and pastrami, apfelstrüdel and ice-cream sodas. Wooden benches outside for *summer* eating. *LD open to 22.00. Closed Sun.* A.Ax.Dc.V. **£**

KOREAN
Arirang 4 D2

31-32 Poland St W1. 0171-437 9662. Large menu may include kim chee (hot pickled cabbage), yuk kwe (beef strips with pear). Sake and ginseng to drink. *LD (Reserve) open to 22.30. Closed Sun.* A.Ax.Dc.V. **£££**

Shilla 4 D2

58-69 Great Marlborough St W1. 0171-434 1650. Charming service to help you with the speciality here – barbecue dishes. Delicious sauces accompany beef, chicken or seafood. Set menus available. *LD open to 22.30.* A.Ax.Dc.V. **££**

MEXICAN
La Cucaracha 4 E2

12-13 Greek St W1. 0171-734 2253. London's first Mexican restaurant, in the cellars of a converted monastery. Hacienda-style decor with a sunny covered terrace at the back. Ceviche, tacos, burritos, enchiladas. *LD open to 23.30. Closed Sun.* V. **££**

Los Locos 4 F3

24 Russell St WC2. 0171-379 0220. Also at 14 Soho St W1 (**4 E2**). 0171-287 0005. Mexican bar and restaurant with lots of Tex-Mex specials. Nachos, tacos, carnitas, steaks, enchiladas, fajitas cooked over mesquite wood. Mexican beers and cock-tails. Disco from *23.30 every night. D open to 21.30, dancing to 03.00.* A.Ax.Dc.V. **££**

MODERN EUROPEAN
Alastair Little 4 E2

49 Frith St W1. 0171-734 5183. Fashionable restaurant with an imaginative, frequently changing menu. Tempting, delicious results such as fish soup, noisettes of lamb with exotic fungi. *LD (Reserve) open to 23.30. Closed Sat L & Sun.* A.V. **£££+**

Atlantic Bar & Grill 4 D3

20 Glasshouse St W1. 0171-734 4888. Glamorous and fash-ionable. Sweep down the wave of stairs to the cavernous art nouveau style dining room. Menu of light dishes, mixed plat-ters and main dishes. *D open to 23.30, to 22.30 Sun. Bar open to 03.00, to 23.30 Sun.*

Bibendum   6 E2
81 Fulham Rd SW3. 0171-581 5817. Delightful restaurant within the unusual 1910 Michelin building. Simple, elegant and inventive French and English dishes. Carefully chosen wine list. *LD (Reserve) open to 23.00, to 22.15 Sun.* A.Ax.V. **£££**+

Langan's Brasserie   4 C4
Stratton St W1. 0171-493 6437. Buzzing atmosphere and stylish surroundings. Changing menu may include oyster mushrooms, soufflé with anchovies, black pudding. Live music *every night. LD open to 23.45, to 24.00 Sat. Closed Sat L & Sun.* A.Ax.Dc.V. **£££**

OPEN-AIR EATING
Barbican, Waterside Café   2 E6
Level 5, Barbican Centre EC2. 0171-638 4141. Modern self-service café by the man-made lake of the arts centre. Snacks or full meals. *LD open to 20.00.* A.Ax.Dc.V. **£-££**

Dan's   6 E3
119 Sydney St SW3. 0171-352 2718. Bright, airy room with hanging plants and seating in a rear garden. English and French cuisine. *LD open to 22.30. Closed Sat L & Sun.* A.Ax.Dc.V. *L* **££** *D* **£££**

La Famiglia   6 C4
7 Langton St SW10. 0171-351 0761. Attractive, with pretty rear garden and southern Italian cooking. Fourteen types of pasta. Italian wines. *LD open to 24.00.* A.Ax.Dc.V. **£££**+

SCANDINAVIAN
Anna's Place
90 Mildmay Park N1. 0171-249 9379. Small, intimate restaurant in Anna's home serving excellent Scandinavian and French food. Camembert with parsley, gravadlax, beef or herring. *LD (Reserve) open to 22.45. Closed Sun & Mon.* No credit cards. **££**

Garbo's   1 B6
42 Crawford St W1. 0171-262 6582. Also at 14 Little Chester St SW1 (**4 C6**). 0171-245 1224. Pleasant restaurant serving Scandinavian home cooking. Herring salad Baltic, cabbage stuffed with minced pork, beef and rice or smoked eel. Imported Swedish beers and Schnapps. *LD (Reserve) open to 23.30. Closed Sat L & Sun L.* A.Ax.V. **££**

SOUTH EAST ASIAN
Lemongrass   1 E1
243 Royal College St NW1. 0171-284 1116. An eclectic restaurant serving Vietnamese, Thai, Cambodian and Chinese dishes. *LD open to 22.45. Closed Sat L & Sun L.* A.V. **££**

Rasa Sayang 4 E2
10 Frith St W1. 0171-734 8720. Unpretentious restaurant offering authentic Singaporean, Indonesian and Malaysian food. Try the beef satay, prawns, gado gado. *LD (Reserve D) open to 23.30. Closed Sat L.* A.Ax.Dc.V. **££**

SPANISH & PORTUGUESE
Caravela 3 F6
39 Beauchamp Place SW3. 0171-581 2366. Small, intimate basement Portuguese restaurant. The menu is largely seafood, with fresh grilled sardines, prawns piri piri and regional specialities. Wine list exclusively Portuguese. Live music in the *evening. LD (Reserve) open to 00.45, to 23.30 Sun.* A.Ax.Dc.V. **££**

Valencia 6 A4
1 Empress Approach, Lillie Rd SW6. 0171-385 0039. London's oldest Spanish restaurant. Large menu of regional dishes and wine list strong on Rioja and Catalan wines. Guitarist *every night. D open to 00.15.* A.V. **££**

THAI
Bahn Thai 4 E2
21a Frith St W1. 0171-437 8504. Stylish decor and high-quality authentic Thai food make this a popular restaurant where the dishes are chilli-rated for spiciness! Vegetarians well catered for. Fiery Thai whisky to drink. *LD (Reserve) open to 23.15, to 22.30 Sun.* A.Ax.V. **££**

Blue Elephant 6 A5
4-5 Fulham Broadway SW6. 0171-385 6595. One of London's best Thai restaurants. The surroundings resemble a tropical jungle, the perfect backdrop for excellent, beautifully prepared dishes presented by waiters in Thai costume. Excellent vegetarian menu. *LD (Reserve) open to 00.30, to 22.30 Sun.* A.Ax.Dc.V. **£££+**

Busabong Too 6 C4
1a Langton St SW10. 0171-352 7414. Low tables and cushions to sit on. Very pleasant, attentive service. Fisherman's soup, beef satay, mint pork with water chestnuts. *LD (Reserve) open to 23.15.* A.Ax.Dc.V. **££**

VEGETARIAN & WHOLEFOOD
Many restaurants now cater for vegetarian tastes, with a variety of dishes on their menus. Below are two specialist establishments:
Cranks 4 D2
37 Marshall St W1. 0171-437 9431. The original London healthfood restaurant. Hot and cold vegetable dishes, soups, pies, salads, cakes, bread, and fruit juices. Licensed. Other branches. *LD (Reserve D) open to 20.00..* A.V. **£**

Diwana Bhel-Poori House   **1 E5**
121 Drummond St NW1. 0171-387 5556. Also at 50 Westbourne Grove W2 (**3 C2**). 0171-221 0721. Indian vegetarian food at very reasonable prices. Samosas, thalis, bhajis. *LD open to 01.00. Closed Mon.* A.Dc.V. **£**

VIETNAMESE
Bonjour Vietnam   **6 A5**
One of the Zen chain of restaurants. A huge 30ft fish tank is part of the relaxed, welcoming atmosphere. Sample traditional and new-wave Vietnamese dishes such as Saigon spicy chicken with chilli or steamed scallops. *LD open to 23.15, to 23.00 Sun.* A.Ax.Dc.V. **££**

Mekong   **7 C2**
46 Churton St SW1. 0171-630 9568. Sample a blend of Vietnamese and Chinese cuisine in this simple restaurant. Spring rolls, beef with lemon grass and a variety of vegetarian dishes. Set menus. *LD (Reserve) open to 22.15.* A.V. **££**

Breakfast and brunch

Price symbols for this section only are as follows: **£** *under £5.00;* **££** *£5.00-£8.00;* **£££** *over £8.00.*

CAFÉS
Bar Italia   **4 E2**
22 Frith St W1. 0171-437 4520. Authentic Italian café, serving breakfast all day. *Open 24 hrs Mon-Sun.* No credit cards. **£**

Gambarti   **2 B5**
38 Lamb's Conduit St WC1. 0171-405 7950. English and Continental breakfasts. Fresh Italian coffee. *Opens 07.00. Closed Sat & Sun.* No credit cards. **£**

Pasticceria Cappucetto   **4 E2**
8-9 Moor St, off Charing Cross Rd W1. 0171-437 9472. Continental pâtisserie. *Opens 07.30 (08.30 Sun).* No credit cards. **£**

Le Tire Bouchon   **4 D3**
6 Upper James St W1. 0171-437 5348. Continental breakfast. *Open 08.30-21.15. Closed Sat & Sun.* A.Ax.Dc.V. **££**

HOTELS
Claridge's   **4 C3**
Brook St W1. 0171-629 8860. English, à la carte or Continental. *Served 07.30-10.30 (08.00-11.00 Sun).* A.Ax.Dc.V. **£££**

Hyde Park Hotel   **4 A5**
66 Knightsbridge SW1. 0171-235 2000. English, à la carte or Continental. *Served 07.00 (08.00 Sun & Bank hols)-10.30.* A.Ax.Dc.V. **£££**

Ritz   **4 D4**
Piccadilly W1. 0171-493 8181. English, à la carte or Continental. *Served 07.00 (08.00 Sat & Sun)-10.30.* A.Ax.Dc.V. **£££**

Savoy 4 G3
Strand WC2. 0171-836 4343. English, Continental or fitness breakfast. *Served 07.00 (08.00 Sun)-10.30.* A.Ax.Dc.V. **£££**

Afternoon tea

Afternoon tea is a British institution; at one time very fashionable, sociable and leisurely. This list gives some of the remaining strongholds. Prices can vary but you should not normally expect to pay more than £12.00 for a full tea. Most will cost between £5.00-£10.00.

HOTELS
Brown's 4 D3
Dover St W1. 0171-493 6020. Very English, country house setting. Sandwiches, cakes, muffins. *Served 15.00-18.00.*
Claridge's 4 C3
Brook St W1. 0171-629 8860. A touch of class in the comfortable reading room. Sandwiches, assorted pastries, cakes. *Served 15.00-17.30 (Reserve).*
Dorchester 4 B4
Park Lane W1. 0171-629 8888. Dainty sandwiches, cakes and pastries in opulent surroundings. *Served 15.00-18.00.*
Ritz 4 D4
Piccadilly W1. 0171-493 8181. Tea in the Palm Court, with dainty sandwiches, pastries and cream cakes. *Served 15.00 & 16.30 (Reserve).*

DEPARTMENT STORES
Most large department stores provide afternoon tea but the following are among the best:
Fortnum & Mason 4 D4
181 Piccadilly W1. 0171-734 8040. Afternoon tea is available at two locations in the store *Mon-Sat.* St James's Restaurant serves a set tea of sandwiches, scones, cake, tea or coffee to a piano accompaniment *15.00-17.20.* The Soda Fountain offers an à la carte tea menu *14.30-17.30.*
Harrods Georgian Restaurant 3 G6
Knightsbridge SW1. 0171-730 1234. Enjoy tea, sandwiches, coffee or fruit juice with bread and butter, scones, cakes and pastries; *served from 15.30.* Alternatively have tea on the Terrace; *served from 15.00.*

CAFÉS
Maison Bouquillon 3 C3
41 Moscow Rd W2. 0171-727 0373. Over 50 varieties of cream cakes and pastries. Also hot savoury dishes, croissants. *Open 08.30-21.00 Mon-Sat, to 20.00 Sun.* No credit cards.

Maison Sagne   **1 C6**
105 Marylebone High St W1. 0171-935 6240. Traditional tea
shop with its own bakery and delicious pâtisserie. Coffee and
croissants, lunches and teas. *Open 08.00-19.00 Mon-Fri,
08.00-18.00 Sat, 09.00-18.00 Sun.* No credit cards.

Pâtisserie Valerie   **4 E3**
44 Old Compton St W1. 0171-437 3466. Long-established
Soho pâtisserie. Tea, coffee and hot chocolate accompany
superb cakes and sandwiches. *Open 08.00-20.00 Mon-Fri,
08.00-19.00 Sat, 10.00-18.00 Sun.* No credit cards.

THÉ DANSANT
Waldorf Hotel   **4 G3**
Aldwych WC2. 0171-836 2400. Opulent Palm Court tea lounge
with comfort and good service. Edwardian elegance. Dancing
to the band and full set tea *Sat & Sun 15.30-18.00 (Reserve).*

Brasseries

Here is a selection of establishments serving food all day
(from breakfast to full meals):

La Brasserie   **3 F6**
272 Brompton Rd SW3. 0171-584 1668. Probably one of the
closest things to a real French brasserie in London.
Conventional menu with omelettes, croque monsieur; also
breakfast and pâtisseries. *Open 08.00-24.00 Mon-Sat, 10.00-
23.30 Sun.* A.Ax.Dc.V. **£££**

Covent Garden Brasserie   **4 F3**
1 Covent Garden Piazza WC2. 0171-240 6654. Relaxed
atmosphere at this Parisian style brasserie. Breakfast and
afternoon tea as well as light meals and more substantial
dishes. *Open 09.00-23.00.* A.Ax.Dc.V. **££**

The Dôme   **6 D4**
354 King's Rd SW3. 0171-352 7611. One of a chain of French-
style brasseries based on the Paris Dôme. Coffee, wine,
spirits, beer and good food. *Open 08.00-23.00 Mon-Sat, 09.00-
22.30 Sun.* A.Ax.Dc.V. **££**

Soho Soho   **4 E2**
11-13 Frith St W1. 0171-494 3491. A brasserie/wine bar with a
selection of good value wines. Brasserie offers typical French
menu with croque monsieur etc; Rôtisserie downstairs offers
grills and snacks all day. *Open 12.00-01.00. Closed Sun.*
A.Ax.Dc.V. **££**

Tuttons Brasserie   **4 F3**
11-12 Russell St WC2. 0171-836 4141. Right on the edge of
Covent Garden Piazza, this is a large, airy brasserie with a
relaxed atmosphere. Good, reasonably priced English/interna-
tional menu. *Open 09.30-23.30 Mon-Thur & Sun, to 24.00 Fri
& Sat.* A.Ax.Dc.V. **£**

Wine bars

Most wine bars are open traditional pub hours: 11.00/11.30-15.00 & 17.30-23.00 Mon-Sat; 12.00-14.00 & 19.00-22.30 Sun. *Some are open all day:* 11.00-23.00 Mon-Sat; 12.00-14.00 & 19.00-22.30 Sun. *These are denoted by* 🍷. *Very few wine bars open all day on Sun.*
Most offer cold food all day, and bar food at designated times at lunchtime and in the evening.
L = 12.00/12.30-14.30/15.00.
D = 18.00-22.30/23.00.
all day = throughout the day from lunchtime to last orders in the evening.
Nicholson's London Pub Guide *gives more detailed information on brasseries and wine bars in the capital.*

🍷 Archduke   5 B4
Concert Hall Approach, South Bank SE1. 0171-928 9370. Nestling underneath the arches near Waterloo Station, with pleasant green decor, live jazz *Thur & Sat,* and good food. *L D.*

🍷 L'Artiste Musclé   4 C4
1 Shepherd Market W1. 0171-493 6150. Informal French wine bar. Good food with daily specials chalked up on the blackboard. Reasonably priced, mainly French, wines. Tables outside in *summer. L D.*

Balls Bros
One of the oldest wine bar chains in London. Very popular, with most of its branches in the City. Over 60 wines on their list, plus wines by the glass. All the following serve food *lunchtime* and *evening.* NB: All branches *close early at 21.00 and are closed Sat & Sun.* The following is only a selection:

6 Cheapside EC2. 0171-248 2708.	5 D2
3 Budge Row, Cannon St EC4. 0171-248 7557. *L only*	5 D2
🍷Hay's Galleria, Tooley St SE1. 0171-407 4301.	5 F4
St Mary-at-Hill EC3. 0171-626 0321.	5 F3
Moor House, London Wall EC2. 0171-628 3944.	5 E1
42 Threadneedle St EC2. 0171-628 3850.	5 E2

🍷 Bill Bentley's Wine Bar   3 G6
31 Beauchamp Place SW3. 0171-588 5080. Dark, cosy bar with an old-fashioned interior and an excellent fish restaurant upstairs. Snacks from the oyster bar and a reasonably priced wine list. *L. Closed Sun.*

🍷 Bow Wine Vaults   5 D2
10 Bow Churchyard EC4. 0171-248 1121. Victorian bar within the sound of Bow Bells. Popular with City gents, with a good selection of over 100 French, Californian, Spanish and German wines. Imaginative food. *L only.* Bar snacks area with free snacks *from 17.30-20.00. Closed Sat & Sun.*

🍺 **Brahms & Liszt** 4 F3

19 Russell St WC2. 0171-240 3661. Lively, crowded wine bar with loud music and a friendly atmosphere. Good food and a reasonable selection of wines. Food *all day.*

Café des Amis du Vin 4 F3

11-14 Hanover Place WC2. 0171-379 3444. Close to the Royal Opera House and always busy. Good range of French, German and Spanish wines accompanied by an inventive menu. *L D. Closed Sun.*

Cork & Bottle 4 E3

44-46 Cranbourn St WC2. 0171-734 7807. Spacious basement wine bar with an unusual variety of quality wines. *L D.*

🍺 **Crusting Pipe** 4 F3

27 Covent Garden Piazza WC2. 0171-836 1415. Part of the Davy's chain. Very popular with seating outside under the piazza canopy. Grills and daily specials in the restaurant and very friendly, helpful service. Food *all day*

Davy's Wine Bars

Old prints and sawdust-covered floors create a bygone Victorian image in these wine bars, the names of which date back to the wine trade of 100 years ago. NB: Most branches *close early at around 20.30 and are closed Sat & Sun.* The following is only a selection:

Boot & Flogger 5 D5

10-20 Redcross Way SE1. 0171 407 1184. Food *all day.*

Bung Hole 4 G1

57 High Holborn WC1. 0171-242 4318. *L.*

City Boot 5 E1

7 Moorfields High Walk EC2. 0171-628 2360. *L.*

Dover Street Wine Bar 4 C3

8-9 Dover St W1. 0171-629 9813. A basement wine bar with a friendly atmosphere and a very good selection of wines. Live music *six nights a week. L D to 01.30. Open to 03.00. Closed Sat L & Sun*

🍺 **Ebury Wine Bar** 7 A2

139 Ebury St SW1. 0171-730 5447. Crowded and cramped, but with a pleasant atmosphere. Comprehensive wine list. *L D.*

🍺 **Gordon's** 4 F4

47 Villiers St WC2. 0171-930 1408. 300-year-old wine bar in curved, cavernous undervaults. Excellent selection of wines and sherries. Good food. *L D.*

🍺 **Shampers** 4 D3

4 Kingly St W1. 0171-437 1692. A brasserie and wine bar with a congenial atmosphere and fine selection of wines. Good, imaginative menu. *L D.* Closed Sun.

El Vino 5 B2

47 Fleet St EC4. 0171-353 6786. Something of an institution.

Thoroughly masculine atmosphere popular with local lawyers and still adhering to a dress code – men in jacket and tie. Long and famous wine list. *L. Open to 20.00. Closed Sat & Sun.*

Pubs

Some pubs still operate under traditional opening hours: 11.00/11.30-15.00 & 17.30-23.00 Mon-Sat; 12.00-14.00 & 19.00-22.30 Sun. *Most are open all day* 11.00-23.00 Mon-Sat; *and* 12.00-14.00 & 19.00-22.30 Sun. *These are denoted by* 🍺. *You may find that some pubs do stay open all day on Sun. Most pubs serve sandwiches and cold snacks all day, but hot food at designated times at lunchtime and in the evening. In the following section:*
Bar food = ploughmans, salads, sandwiches, pies, lasagne. Restaurant = three-course menu and more substantial dishes. L = 12.30-14.30. D = 17.30-21.00/22.00. Nicholson's London Pub Guide *gives more detailed information on where to drink in the capital.*

The Cartoonist 5 B2
76 Shoe Lane EC4. 0171-353 2828. In the heart of the old newspaper world, this Victorian pub is the headquarters of the International Cartoonist Club. *Bar food L. Closed Sat & Sun.*

🍺 Cheshire Cheese 5 B3
5 Little Essex St WC2. 0171-836 2347. Intimate Jacobean pub with original beams and three bars. Regulars come from the nearby Law Courts and it is reputedly haunted by an unfriendly ghost! *Bar food L. Closed Sat & Sun.*

🍺 Dirty Dick's 5 F2
202 Bishopsgate EC2. 0171-283 5888. The original pub named after Nat Bentley, well-known 18thC miser of the ballad. The cobwebs, stuffed cats and other detritus have since been removed with the remnants preserved behind glass. Now fully refurbished and serving real ales. *Bar food L. Restaurant L. Closed Sat LD & Sun D.*

The Flask
77 Highgate West Hill N6. 0181-340 7260. Famous 17thC tavern named after the flasks bought here and filled at the Hampstead wells. Dick Turpin once hid in the cellars. Former patrons include Hogarth and Karl Marx. *Bar food L D. Restaurant L.*

🍺 French House 4 E2
49 Dean St W1. 0171-437 2799. Refuge for the Free French during World War II. De Gaulle drank here, as have Maurice Chevalier, Brendan Behan and Dylan Thomas. Excellent choice of wines and champagnes. *Bar food L D. Restaurant L D.*

🍺 George Inn   **5 D5**
77 Borough High St SE1. 0171-407 2056. Unique galleried
coaching inn rebuilt 1676 and featured in Dickens' *Little Dorrit.*
Courtyard entertainment (usually Morris dancing) in *summer.*
Bar food L D. Restaurant L D.

Holly Bush
22 Holly Mount, off Heath St NW3. 0171-435 2892.
Picturesque and rambling pub dating to 1796. Unchanged
atmosphere prevails with gas lamps and a dark, sagging
ceiling. *Bar food L.*

Island Queen   **2 D3**
87 Noel Rd N1. 0171-226 5507. Looming papier mâché figures
dominate the bar in this popular local. Pool room and restaurant. *Bar food L.*

The Lamb   **2 B5**
94 Lamb's Conduit St WC1. 0171-405 0713. A busy
Bloomsbury local with some intriguing music-hall photographs
and Hogarth prints. Original snob-screens. *Bar food L.*
Restaurant Sun L.

🍺 Lamb & Flag   **4 F3**
33 Rose St WC2. 0171-497 9504. 300-year-old pub once nicknamed the 'Bucket of Blood' because of the occurrence of
bare fist fights. Now a popular, mellow bar. Fine range of
cheeses. *Bar food L.*

Old Bull & Bush
North End Way NW3. 0181-455 3685. The famous pub of the
Florrie Forde song. Drink on the forecourt and gaze at
Hampstead Heath opposite. *Bar food L. Restaurant L.*

Running Footman   **4 C4**
5 Charles St W1. 0171-499 2988. Once had the longest name in
London, 'I am the only Running Footman' (after the men who
used to run before carriages, clearing the way and paying the
tolls). Popular with nearby workers. *Bar food L D. Restaurant D.*

🍺 The Salisbury   **4 F3**
90 St Martin's Lane WC2. 0171-836 5863. Glittering
Edwardian pub in the heart of theatreland. Cut-glass mirrors
and first-class hot and cold buffet. Famous meeting place for
theatre people. *Bar food L D.*

Seven Stars   **5 B2**
53 Carey St WC2. 0171-242 8521. Behind the Law Courts stands
this early 17thC pub, one of the smallest in London. *Bar food L.*

🍺 Sherlock Holmes   **4 F4**
10 Northumberland St WC2. 0171-930 2644. Great selection
of real ales and a restaurant serving traditional English food.
Upstairs is a perfect replica of Holmes' study at 221b Baker
St. *Bar food L D.*

🍺 Spaniard's Inn
Spaniard's Rd NW3. 0181-455 3276. Famous 16thC inn with literary and Dick Turpin associations. Pretty garden. *Bar food L D.*

Still & Star   **5 G2**
1 Little Somerset St (off Mansell St) E1. 0171-488 3761. The
only one of its name in England, and set in 'blood alley' where
Jack the Ripper struck. *Bar food L. Closed Sat & Sun.*

RIVERSIDE PUBS
🍺 The Anchor   **5 C3**
Bankside SE1. 0171-407 1577. 18thC replacement of original
destroyed by Great Fire of 1666. Exposed beams, large open
fireplace. *Bar food L D. Restaurant L D (Reserve).*
The Angel
101 Bermondsey Wall East SE16. 0171-237 3608. 15thC
Thames-side pub with extensive views of Tower Bridge, the
City and the Pool of London. Famous former imbibers include
Samuel Pepys, Captain Cook and Laurel and Hardy. *Bar food L
(not Sat) D. Restaurant L (not Sat) D. Closed Sun eve.*
Bull's Head
Strand-on-the-Green   W4.   0181-994   0647.   350-year-old
Chiswick waterfront tavern. Cromwell was nearly caught here
by the Royalists. Sheltered beer garden and terrace. *Bar food
L D . Restaurant LD.*
🍺 Cutty Sark
Ballast Quay, Lassell St SE10. 0181-858 3146. Quiet Georgian
pub with wooden interior. Overlooks the river and wharves
near *Cutty Sark* in dry dock. *Bar food L.*
🍺 Dickens Inn   **5 G4**
St Katharine's Way E1. 0171-488 1226. Converted historic
warehouse with fine views of the diverse craft in St
Katharine's Dock marina. Outside eating in *summer*. Two
restaurants. *Bar food L D. Restaurant L D.*
🍺 The Dove
19 Upper Mall W6. 0181-748 5405. Mellow 18thC pub with
terrace overlooking the river. Graham Greene and Ernest
Hemingway drank here. Has the smallest bar room, which
has earned it an entry in the *Guinness Book of Records. Bar
food L. Restaurant L.*
London Apprentice
62 Church St, Old Isleworth, Middx. 0181-560 1915. Famous
16thC pub with fine Elizabethan and Georgian interiors. *Bar
food L. Restaurant D.*
🍺 The Mayflower
117 Rotherhithe St SE16. 0171-237 4088. Partially rebuilt
Tudor inn named after the ship in which the Pilgrim Fathers
reached America. The only pub in England licensed to sell
British and American stamps. Drink on the jetty in good
weather. *Bar food L D. Restaurant L D.*
Prospect of Whitby
57 Wapping Wall E1. 0171-481 1095. Historic dockland tavern
dating back to the reign of Henry VIII. Samuel Pepys drank

here, as did 'hanging' Judge Jeffreys. Decorated with nautical souvenirs and fine pewter. Restaurant overlooking the river. *Bar food L D. Restaurant L D.*

MUSIC PUBS

These vary enormously, from pubs with a pianist playing old favourites, to those with large audience space for live bands. The pubs listed below are established live music venues. It's always advisable to check listings in advance to find out what is on. Most pubs with a separate music room charge an entry fee, though it is rarely more than £5.00 and often less.

Bull & Gate

389 Kentish Town Rd NW5. 0171-485 5358. Mainly indie and rock. *Evenings Mon-Sun. Bar food L.*

🍵 Bull's Head

373 Lonsdale Rd SW13. 0181-876 5241. Mainstream modern jazz by top English and international musicians. *Evenings Mon-Sun & Sun lunchtime. Bar food L. Restaurant L (Sun only) D.*

Half Moon

93 Lower Richmond Rd SW15. 0181-780 9383. Jazz, R & B, rock, folk and soul in separate back room. Occasional top names. *Bar food D.*

Swan Tavern   6 A5

1 Fulham Broadway SW6. 0171-385 1840. Mixed bands and R & B. *Evenings Mon-Sun & Sun lunchtime. Bar food D.*

Water Rats   2 A4

328 Grays Inn Rd WC1. 0171-837 7269. Influential venue. Indie hopefuls, ex punk bands, major label bands. Full of A&R men. *Evenings Mon-Sun.*

THEATRE PUBS

The Gate   3 B3

Prince Albert Pub, 11 Pembridge Rd W11. 0171-229 0706. New works, adaptations of novels and revivals of lesser known plays by important writers. Performances *Mon-Sat.*

King's Head   2 D3

115 Upper St N1. 0171-226 1916. Probably the best known and most widely reviewed of the theatre pubs. Decorated with theatre bills. You can have a meal before the show and stay at your table for the performance. Also live music. Performances *Mon-Sun. Bar food L. Restaurant D.* **(M)**

Man in the Moon   6 D4

392 King's Rd SW3. 0171-351 2876. A purpose-built studio presenting modern plays. The pub is worth a visit in its own right. Performances *Tue-Sun.* **(M)**

ENTERTAINMENT

For more detailed information see Nicholson's London Nightlife Guide. *See page 127 for a map of West End theatres and cinemas.*
Artsline: *0171-388 2227 offers free advice and information on access to arts and entertainment for disabled people.*
Evening Standard Theatrecall & Entertainment Guide: *(0839) 200002 gives previews and booking information. Calls cost 39p per minute cheap rate and 49p per minute at other times.*

Theatre ticket agencies

Fenchurch Booking Agency   5 D4
94 Southwark St SE1. 0171-928 8585. A.V.
First Call
0171-240 1000. A.Ax.Dc.V.
Keith Prowse
0171-420 0000. A.Ax.Dc.V.
Society of London Theatre Half-Price   4 E3
Ticket Booth (SOLT)
Leicester Sq WC2. Unsold tickets at half price on the day of the performance from the pavilion on the south side of Leicester Square. *Open from 12.00* (for matinées) *& 14.30-18.30* (for evening performances). Maximum 4 tickets. No credit cards.
Ticketmaster UK Ltd   4 E3
48 Leicester Sq WC2. 0171-344 4444. A.Ax.V.

Theatres

Adelphi   4 F3
Strand WC2. 0171-344 0055. Musicals.
Albery   4 F3
St Martin's Lane WC2. 0171-369 1730. Originally the New Theatre. Renamed in 1973. Musicals, comedy and drama.
Aldwych   4 G3
Aldwych WC2. 0171-836 6404. Former London home of the Royal Shakespeare Company. Plays, comedies and musicals.
Ambassadors   4 E3
West St WC2. 0171-836 6111. Small theatre, the original home of *The Mousetrap* until it moved to the nearby St Martin's.
Apollo   4 E3
Shaftesbury Ave W1. 0171-494 5070. Old tradition of musical comedy. Now presents musicals, comedy and drama.

Apollo Victoria   4 C6
17 Wilton Rd SW1. 0171-828 8665. This auditorium was completely transformed to accommodate the hit rollerskating railway musical *Starlight Express*.

Barbican   2 E6
Barbican Centre, Silk St EC2. 0171-638 8891. Purpose-built for the Royal Shakespeare Company; the main auditorium is for large-scale productions in repertory and the Pit, a smaller studio theatre, is for new works.

Comedy   4 E3
Panton St SW1. 0171-867 1045. Good intimate theatre showing small-cast plays.

Criterion   4 E3
Piccadilly Circus W1. 0171-839 8811. Listed building which has undergone extensive renovations. Houses the only underground auditorium in London.

Donmar Warehouse   4 F2
41 Earlham St WC2. 0171-867 1150. Tiny theatre showing small productions. *Closure threatened at time of going to press.*

Drury Lane (Theatre Royal)   4 G3
Catherine St WC2. 0171-494 5062. Operated under Royal Charter by Thomas Kiligrew in 1663, it has been burnt or pulled down and rebuilt four times. Nell Gwynne performed here and Orange Moll sold her oranges. Garrick, Mrs Siddons, Kean and others played here. General policy now is vast musical productions like *Miss Saigon*.

Duchess   4 G3
Catherine St WC2. 0171-494 5075. Opened 1929. Plays, serious drama, light comedy and musicals.

Duke of York's   4 F3
St Martin's Lane WC2. 0171-836 5122. Built by 'Mad (Violet) Melnotte' in 1892. Associated with names like Frohman, George Bernard Shaw, Granville Barker, Chaplin and the Ballet Rambert. *Royal Court productions will be staged here during renovations.*

Fortune   4 F3
Russell St WC2. 0171-836 2238. Small compared with its neighbour, Drury Lane. Intimate revues (Peter Cook and Dudley Moore shot to fame here in *Beyond the Fringe*), musicals and modern drama.

Garrick   4 E2
Charing Cross Rd WC2. 0171-494 5085. Built 1897. Notable managers included Bouchier and Jack Buchanan. Drama and comedies.

Gielgud   4 E3
Shaftesbury Ave W1. 0171-494 5065. Renamed in honour of Sir John Gielgud. A wide variety of successful plays and comedies.

Greenwich
Crooms Hill SE10. 0181-858 7755. Stages a season of plays including new works, revivals and classics, often with famous names in the cast. Bar and good restaurant.

Haymarket (Theatre Royal)   4 E3
Haymarket SW1. 0171-930 8800. Originally built in 1721 as the Little Theatre in the Hay, it became Royal 50 years later. The present theatre was built by Nash in 1821 and is sometimes enlivened by the ghost of Mr Buckstone, Queen Victoria's favourite actor-manager. He no doubt approves of the policy to present plays of quality.

Her Majesty's   4 E3
Haymarket SW1. 0171-494 5400. A fine Victorian baroque theatre founded by Beerbohm Tree. Successes include *West Side Story, Fiddler on the Roof, Amadeus* and, most recently, Lloyd Webber's *Phantom of the Opera.*

Lyric   4 E3
Shaftesbury Ave W1. 0171-494 5045. Oldest theatre in Shaftesbury Avenue (built 1888). Eleonora Duse, Sarah Bernhardt, Owen Nares and Tallulah Bankhead all had long runs here. Musicals and plays.

Lyric Hammersmith
King St W6. 0181-741 2311. Rebuilt and restored to original Victorian splendour inside a modern shell. Spacious foyers, bar, restaurant and terrace. Wide-ranging productions.

Mermaid   5 C3
Puddle Dock, Blackfriars EC4. 0171-236 2211. Plays and musicals. Restaurant and two bars overlooking the Thames.

New London   4 F2
Drury Lane WC2. 0171-405 0072. Can convert from a 900-seat conventional theatre to an intimate theatre-in-the-round within minutes. Built on the site of the old Winter Gardens. The hit musical *Cats* is well-established here.

Old Vic   5 B5
Waterloo Rd SE1. 0171-928 7616. Built 1818. For a long time the home of the National Theatre Company, then housed the Prospect Theatre Company. It now shows plays and musicals amid recreated Victorian decor.

Palace   4 E3
Shaftesbury Ave W1. 0171-434 0909. Listed building. Originally intended by Richard D'Oyly Carte to be the Royal English Opera House, but eventually became the Palace Theatre of Varieties. Staged performances by Pavlova and Nijinski. Now owned by Sir Andrew Lloyd Webber whose musical *Jesus Christ Superstar* enjoyed a record run here; *Les Misérables* is its latest success story.

Phoenix
4 E2
Charing Cross Rd WC2. 0171-867 1044. A large theatre showing comedies, plays and musicals.

Piccadilly
4 D3
Denman St W1. 0171-867 1118. A pre-war theatre which showed the first season of 'Talkies' in Britain. Varied post-war history of light comedy, plays and musicals. Many Royal Shakespeare Company productions are staged here.

Playhouse
4 F4
Northumberland Ave WC2. 0171-839 4401. Edwardian theatre used as a BBC studio and then closed in 1975. Restored to former glory and re-opened in 1987. Stages musicals, serious drama and comedies.

Prince Edward
4 E3
Old Compton St W1. 0171-734 8951. Started life as the 'London Casino' in 1936, then became a cinema. Now a large theatre staging musicals; the hit show *Evita* ran for 2900 performances here.

Prince of Wales
4 E3
Coventry St W1. 0171-839 5972. Rebuilt 1937, this large, modern theatre has housed many musicals.

Queen's
4 E3
Shaftesbury Ave W1. 0171-494 5040. Very successful between the wars. Still presents good drama and varied productions.

Royal Court
6 F2
Sloane Sq SW1. 0171-730 1745. Home of the English Stage Company, which produces many major new plays. *Productions will transfer to Duke of York's during renovations due to start late 1996.*

Royal National
5 A4
South Bank SE1. 0171-928 2252. Complex of three theatres, the Olivier, Lyttelton and Cottesloe. Home of the National Theatre Company. Stages a wide mixture of plays in repertory, including new works, revivals, Shakespeare and musicals. Also free foyer entertainment. Restaurants, bars, exhibitions.

St Martin's
4 E3
West St WC2. 0171-836 1443. Intimate playhouse with unusual polished teak doors. *The Mousetrap* continues its record run here, having transferred from the Ambassadors.

Savoy
4 G3
Strand WC2. 0171-836 8888. Entrance is in the forecourt of the Savoy Hotel. Produces a variety of plays, comedies and musicals.

Shaftesbury
4 E3
Shaftesbury Ave WC2. 0171-379 5399. Permanent base of the Theatre of Comedy Company.

Strand
4 G3
Aldwych WC2. 0171-930 8800. Large theatre presenting a mixture of straight plays, comedies and musicals.

Vaudeville   **4 F3**
Strand WC2. 0171-836 9987. Listed building which originally
ran farce and burlesque (hence the name).

Victoria Palace   **4 D6**
Victoria St SW1. 0171-834 1317. Musicals, variety shows and
plays. Once home of the Crazy Gang and the *Black and White
Minstrel Show*, the musical *Buddy* is a recent success.

Whitehall   **4 F4**
14 Whitehall SW1. 0171-867 1119. Splendid art deco interior.
Stages varied productions.

Wyndham's   **4 E2**
Charing Cross Rd WC2. 0171-867 1116. Small, pretty and
successful theatre founded by Sir Charles Wyndham, the
famous actor-manager. Plays, comedies and musicals.

Young Vic   **5 B5**
66 The Cut SE1. 0171-938 6363. Young people's repertoire
theatre mainly showing the classics and established modern
plays, but also some new plays and musicals.

Open-air theatre

Various parks stage one-off theatrical events in summer. *To
find out more about these, check* Time Out *and* What's On *or
phone the individual park (see* Out and About *on page 47).*

Holland Park Theatre   **3 A5**
Holland Park W8. 0171-602 7856. 600-seat theatre staging
dance, opera and theatre productions *Jun-Aug*. Canopy covering is a definite attraction given the fickleness of the English
summer! *Phone for times and days.*

Regent's Park Open-Air Theatre   **1 C4**
Inner Circle, Regent's Park NW1. 0171-486 2431. Enclosed
within the park, in a magical setting. Plays by Shakespeare
and others alternate from *May-Sep*. Book in advance.
Performances 20.00 Mon-Sat.

Opera, ballet and dance

London Coliseum   **4 F3**
St Martin's Lane WC2. 0171-836 3161. London's biggest theatre –
2358 seats. A leading national music venue, home of the English
National Opera and a favourite with visiting foreign companies.
Dance and ballet productions are staged in *summer*, opera at
other times. Box office *open 10.00-20.00. Closed Sun.* A.Ax.Dc.V.

The Place   **1 F4**
17 Duke's Rd WC1. 0171-387 0031. The Place presents contemporary dance work of an exciting and experimental nature. It is
home of the Richard Alston Dance Company, Showbana

Jeyasingh Dance Company, Random Dance Company and others. Box office *open 12.00-18.00, or up until time of performance.* A.V.

Royal Opera House   **4 F3**
Covent Garden WC2. 0171-304 4000. Recorded information: 0171-836 6903. Credit card booking: 0898 600001. Home of the Royal Ballet and the Royal Opera Company. Sixty-five tickets are reserved for sale at the box office in Floral St from *10.00* on day of performance only (except for gala performances). If the performance is a sell-out, 50 standing-room tickets are made available in the foyer at *19.00*. Be warned – queues have been known to start at dawn! Box office *open 10.00-20.00. Closed Sun.* A.Ax.Dc.V. *Plans to close for redevelopment in 1997.*

Sadler's Wells   **2 C4**
Rosebery Ave EC1. 0171-278 8916. The first theatre here was a 'musick' house built in 1683 by Thomas Sadler as a side attraction to his medicinal well. Birthplace of the English National Opera, it now stages productions by leading British and international ballet, dance and opera companies. Box office *open 10.30-19.30, or 18.30 if no performance.* A.Ax.V.

Concert halls

Barbican Hall   **2 E6**
Barbican Centre EC1. 0171-638 8891. Base of the London Symphony Orchestra. Three one-month seasons per year. Also used as a venue for opera, jazz and light classical music. Box office *open 09.00-20.00 Mon-Sun.* A.Ax.V.

Central Hall   **4 E5**
Storey's Gate SW1. 0171-222 8010. This ornate building is the Chief Methodist Church, built 1905-11. Large hall seats 2640 and is used for organ recitals and orchestral concerts. Tickets at door or direct from event organisers. *Phone for details.*

Conway Hall   **2 B6**
Red Lion Sq WC1. 0171-242 8032. Two halls, one of which is famous for hosting celebrated *Sun eve* chamber music concerts from *Oct-Apr.* No telephone box office. No credit cards.

Royal Albert Hall   **3 E5**
Kensington Gore SW7. 0171-589 8212. Victorian domed hall used for rock, folk and jazz but especially for classical concerts. Famous for the annual Promenade concerts from *Jul-Sep* (see page 36). New home of the Royal Philharmonic Orchestra. Box office *open 09.00-21.00 Mon-Sun.* A.Ax.V.

Royal Festival Hall   **5 A4**
South Bank SE1. 0171-928 8800. Built in 1951 for the Festival of Britain, it seats 3000 and hosts mainly choral and orchestral concerts. Box office *open 10.00-21.00 Mon-Sun.* A.Ax.Dc.V.

RFH2 (Queen Elizabeth Hall) **5 A4**
South Bank SE1. 0171-928 8800. Shares a foyer with the
Purcell Room. Seats 1100, and usually stages chamber music,
small orchestral concerts or solo recitals. Also opera and
dance. Box office *open 10.00-21.00 Mon-Sun.* A.Ax.Dc.V.

RFH3 (Purcell Room) **5 A4**
South Bank SE1. 0171-928 8800. Smallest of the three South
Bank concert halls. Popular and ideal for chamber music and solo
concerts. Box office *open 10.00-21.00 Mon-Sun.* A.Ax.Dc.V.

Wigmore Hall **4 C2**
36 Wigmore St W1. 0171-935 2141. Excellent acoustics and
intimate atmosphere. Popular coffee concerts *11.30 Sun.*
Stages instrumental, song, chamber music and solo recitals.
Seats 540. Box office *open 10.00-20.30 Mon-Sat (telephone
bookings until 19.00).* A.Ax.Dc.V.

Dinner and entertainment

*Dine in elegant surroundings with cabaret entertainment and
dancing at one of the following venues. Book in advance.*

Barbarellas Restaurant **6 B5**
428 Fulham Rd SW6. 0171-385 9434. Cascading fountains,
plus a stylish, sophisticated disco. Unusual Italian menu.
D open to 03.00. Closed Sun. A.Ax.Dc.V. **£££**

L'Hirondelle **4 D3**
99-101 Regent St W1 (entrance in Swallow St). 0171-734
1511. Theatre/restaurant with spectacular, glamorous cabaret.
International menu. Live music *from 21.30.* Cabaret *22.45 &
01.00. Open to 02.00. Closed Sun.* A.Ax.Dc.V. **£££**

London Entertains
All reservations 0171-224 9000. Runs special evenings at
three different venues, each with its own distinctive character:
Beefeater by the Tower of London, The Cockney and *The Talk
of London.* All three are operated on advance bookings and are
open according to demand. The price is the same for all, and
includes a four- to five-course meal, unlimited drink and show.
There is a surcharge on *Sat. D (Reserve). Phone for times.*
A.Ax.Dc.V. **£££+**

Royal Garden Hotel, Royal Roof Restaurant **3 C5**
2-24 Kensington High St W8. 0171-937 8000. Modern
European restaurant with dinner dancing *Thur-Sat evening.*
Excellent views over Kensington Palace and Gardens. *Open to
22.30, to 23.00 Sat. Closed Sun.* A.Ax.Dc.V. **£££+**

Savoy (River Restaurant) **4 G3**
Savoy Hotel, Strand WC2. 0171-836 4343. Elegant and formal,
overlooking the Thames. Worldwide and well-deserved
reputation. Dancing to the resident trio. *D open to 23.30. (No
dinner dance on Sun.)* A.Ax.Dc.V. **£££+**

Southamptons 124 and All That Jazz   4 F1
124 Southampton Row WC1. 0171-405 1466. A massive refurbishment of the old Entrecote restaurant brings great jazz and an excellent and varied menu. *Open to 01.30 Mon-Sat, to 24.00 Sun.* A.Ax.V. **££**

Terrace Restaurant   4 B4
Dorchester Hotel, Park Lane W1. 0171-629 8888. Stately dinner dancing in gracious surroundings. French *haute cuisine.* Dinner dances *Fri & Sat.* A.Ax.Dc.V. **£££**

Terrazza Est   5 B2
109 Fleet St EC4. 0171-353 2680. Large basement restaurant known as the Spaghetti Opera for its superb, uplifting opera singing *(from 19.30).* Lively atmosphere. Set and à la carte menus. *Open to 23.00. Closed Sat & Sun.* A.Ax.Dc.V. **£££**+

Windows on the World, Hilton Hotel   4 B4
Park Lane W1. 0171-493 8000. The name is not an exaggeration! Diners are afforded intoxicating views over the city from 28 floors up. International menu. Dance floor, live music. *Open to 02.00.* A.Ax.Dc.V. **£££**

Live music venues

Consult Time Out, What's On *and the music press to check who's playing where, and when.*

The Forum
9-17 Highgate Rd NW5. 0171-284 1001. Formerly the Town & Country Club, this remains one of the best live music venues in London. Box office *open 10.00-18.00 Mon-Sat, 11.30-17.00 Sun.* A.V.

The Grand
St John's Hill SW11. 0171-738 9000. Converted theatre offering indie, rock and reggae. Box office *open 09.30-18.00 Mon-Sat.* A.V.

Hammersmith Apollo
Queen Caroline St W6. 0181-741 4868. Formerly the Hammersmith Odeon, this legendary venue plays host to all kinds of bands. Box office *open 10.00-18.00. Closed Sun.* No credit cards.

Marquee   4 E2
105 Charing Cross Rd WC2. 0171-437 6603. One of London's original rock clubs. Still a popular, lively spot. *Open to 24.00, to 03.00 Thur-Sat, to 22.30 Sun.* Box office *open 10.00-18.00 Mon-Fri, 12.00-18.00 Sat.* A.V.

Mean Fiddler
24-28a Harlesden High St NW10. 0181-961 5490. Stages well-known indie rock bands, plus folk and country & western. Dancing and bar *to 02.00 Sat.* Box office *open 10.00-18.00 Mon-Sat, 11.30-17.00 Sun.* A.V.

100 Club   **4 C2**
100 Oxford St W1. 0171-636 0933. Historically the home of British traditional jazz. Also modern jazz, blues and swing. *Open to 24.00, to 03.00 Fri, to 01.00 Sat.* No box office. No credit cards.

Palookaville   **4 F3**
13a James St WC2. 0171-240 5857. Lively restaurant and wine bar in the heart of Covent Garden. French cuisine accompanied by jazz and blues. *Open to 01.00, to 02.00 Thur-Sat.* A.Ax.Dc.V.

Ronnie Scott's   **4 E2**
47 Frith St W1. 0171-439 0747. Reputedly the best jazz club in Europe. Can be hot and smoky on a busy night, but it's the sounds people come for. Advisable to book in advance. *Open to 03.00.* Box office *open 11.00-18.00 Mon-Fri, 12.30-18.00 Sat, from 19.00 Sun.* A.Ax.Dc.V.

Members-only clubs and casinos

To join an exclusive clientele in a relaxed and well-tended setting, choose one of the members-only nightclubs. Most of these will provide restaurants and entertainment. Be on your guard, however, for those which also offer 'hostesses' – women employed to boost the sales of drinks. Most of them have an expensive taste in champagne and you will have to pay for the pleasure of their company.

*Most clubs will require you to be a member, although short-term membership is usually available for visitors. In some clubs visitors from overseas get reduced rates or free membership. For an annual subscription fee the **Clubman's Club**, 262-264 Regent St St W1 (0171-287 2091), will supply membership and benefits at clubs in Britain and abroad.*

*You can enter a gaming house only as a member or a guest of a member. By law, when you join a gaming club you will not be admitted until you have filled in a declaration of your intent to gamble and 48 hours have elapsed from the time you signed this declaration. The number **(48)** after a club's name means this rule applies.*

(M) *means that membership is necessary for entry.*

Annabel's   **4 C3**
44 Berkeley Sq W1. 0171-629 2350. Legendary haunt of the rich and famous. Past members have included royals, millionaires and showbiz stars. Long waiting list, but you can get a temporary three-week membership if proposed by an existing member. **(M)**. *Open to 03.00. Closed Sun.*

Charlie Chester Casino (48)   **4 E3**
12 Archer St W1. 0171-734 0255. Modern, easy-going nightclub with restaurant and gambling rooms. **(M)**. *Open to 04.00.*

Clermont Club (48)   4 C3
44 Berkeley Sq W1. 0171-493 5587. An 18thC town house, opulent and comfortable. Select and very expensive to join; a favourite with London's well-heeled businessmen. Excellent restaurant with Arabic cuisine. **(M)**. *Open to 04.00.*

Director's Lodge   4 D4
13 Mason's Yard, Duke St SW1. 0171-839 6109. Businessmen's club with hostesses. Restaurant with resident band. Entrance fee. *Open to 03.00. Closed Sat & Sun.*

Morton's   4 C3
28 Berkeley Sq W1. 0171-499 0363. Set in a Victorian town house. Bar and restaurant. Attracts wealthy clientele. **(M)**. *Open to 03.00. Closed Sun.*

Stork Club   4 D3
99 Regent St W1. 0171-734 1393. Luxury restaurant with dance band and spectacular cabaret. *Open to 03.30. Closed Sun.*

Nightclubs and discotheques

These do not require membership and usually host one-night clubs. As these change frequently, it's a good idea to phone the venue or consult Time Out *or* What's On *in advance. Expect to pay £10.00 for entry to most of the following clubs.*

Equinox   4 E3
Leicester Sq WC2. 0171-437 1446. Full of lights, mirrors, staircases and balconies. Enjoyable and friendly. *Open to 03.00 Mon-Thur, to 04.00 Fri & Sat. Closed Sun.* A.Ax.V.

Hippodrome   4 E3
Leicester Sq WC2. 0171-437 4311. A black cave of brass and chrome illuminated by an amazing lighting system. Six bars, restaurant. *Open to 03.00 Mon-Thur, to 03.30 Fri & Sat.* A.Ax.Dc.V.

Limelight   4 E3
136 Shaftesbury Ave W1. 0171-434 0572. Large and lavish club, housed somewhat incongruously in a former Welsh Presbyterian Church. Very popular at weekends. Snack bar. *Open to 03.30. Closed Sun.* A.Ax.Dc.V.

Stringfellows   4 F3
16 Upper St Martin's Lane WC2. 0171-240 5534. Most celebrities have been photographed flashing their teeth and jewellery at Stringfellows, but beware – the rich and famous tend to keep themselves to themselves. A la carte restaurant. *Open to 03.30. Closed Sun.* A.Ax.Dc.V.

The Wag   4 E3
35 Wardour St W1. 0171-437 5534. Attracts an exuberant, young clientele. Weekend nights are very popular. *Open to 03.30, to 06.00 Fri & Sat. Closed Sun.* No credit cards.

EMERGENCY INFORMATION & SERVICES

ACCIDENT/AMBULANCE
If there's an accident or you need an ambulance for any reason, dial **999** and ask for ambulance.

BABYSITTING AND CHILDCARE
Chelsea Baby Hire
51 Lamberhurst Rd SE27. 0181-670 7304. Push-chairs, carrycots, car seats etc from one night onwards. Free delivery and collection (central London). Fully qualified nannies available for babysitting. Free brochure supplied on request.
Universal Aunts
PO Box 304, Clapham SW4. 0171-738 8937. A well-known agency that will provide all kinds of domestic help, including babysitters. Office *open 09.30-17.00 Mon-Fri.*

CAR BREAKDOWN
AA (Automobile Association)
Freephone breakdown service 0800 887766. *24 hrs Mon-Sun.* You can call the AA out if your car breaks down, but you will have to join on the spot if you are not already a member. A.V.
National Breakdown
Freephone breakdown service 0800 400600. *24 hrs Mon-Sun.* Non-members will pay more for rescue/recovery than members. A.V.
Olympic Breakdown Service
0171-624 8662. *24 hrs Mon-Sun.* An AA and RAC-approved recovery service covering the whole of London. A.V.
RAC (Royal Automobile Club)
Freephone 0800 828282. *24 hrs Mon-Sun.* You will need to be a member of the RAC, or join when they arrive. A.Ax.V.

CHEMISTS (Late-night)
The local police station keeps a list of chemists and doctors available at all hours.
Bliss Chemist   **3 G3**
5 Marble Arch W1. 0171-723 6116. *Open 09.00-24.00 every day of the year.* Also at 50-56 Willesden Lane NW6. 0171-624 8000. *Open 09.00-24.00 Mon-Sun.*

Boots 4 E3
Piccadilly Circus W1. 0171-734 6126. *Open 08.30-20.00 Mon-Fri, 09.00-20.00 Sat, 12.00-18.00 Sun.* Also at 75 Queensway W2 (**3 C3**). 0171-229 9266. *Open 09.00-22.00 Mon-Sat, 13.00-22.00 Sun.*

Warman Freed
45 Golders Green Rd NW11. 0181-455 4351. *Open 08.30-24.00 every day of the year.*

CREDIT CARDS
*If you have lost an **Access** or **Visa** card issued by a bank in the UK, contact the emergency number of the issuing bank:*

Barclays
(01604) 230230. *24 hrs.*

Lloyds
(01702) 364364. *24 hrs.*

Midland
0181 450 3122. *24 hrs.*

National Westminster
(0113) 2778899. *24 hrs.*

Royal Bank of Scotland
(01702) 362988. *24 hrs.*

*If you have lost a **Mastercard** or **Visa** card issued abroad, contact the following:*

Mastercard
(01702) 362988. *24 hrs.*

Visa
(01604) 230230. *24 hrs.*

Contact the emergency numbers listed below if you have lost the following cards:

American Express
(01273) 696933. *24 hrs.*

Diners Club
(01252) 516261. *24 hrs.*

Eurocheque card
(0113) 2778899. *24 hrs.*

HOSPITALS
Free medical treatment is available under the National Health Service (NHS) to British citizens, students studying courses of six months or more, people who are working in Britain, EC Nationals and visitors from other countries with reciprocal arrangements. **All** other foreign visitors will be required to pay for medical treatment they receive.

Hospitals with 24-hour casualty departments:
Charing Cross Hospital
Fulham Palace Rd, Hammersmith W6. 0181-846 1234.

Chelsea and Westminster Hospital 6 C4
369 Fulham Rd SW10. 0181-746 8000.

Guy's Hospital   **5 E4**
St Thomas St SE1. 0171-955 5000.
Hammersmith Hospital
Du Cane Rd, Shepherd's Bush W12. 0181-743 2030.
Queen Mary's University Hospital
Roehampton La SW15. 0181-789 6611.
Royal Free Hospital
Pond St, Hampstead NW3. 0171-794 0500.
Royal London Hospital
Whitechapel Rd, Whitechapel E1. 0171-377 7000.
St Thomas's Hospital   **4 G6**
Lambeth Palace Rd SE1. 0171-928 9292.
University College Hospital   **1 F5**
Gower St WC1. 0171-387 9300.
Whittington Hospital
Highgate Hill, Archway N19. 0171-272 3070.

LATE-NIGHT FOOD
Burger King   **4 E3**
17-21 Leicester Sq WC2. No phone. Member of the well-known chain. Burgers, fries and milkshakes. *Open to 04.00, to 23.30 Sun.*
Harry's   **4 D3**
19 Kingly St W1. 0171-434 0309. A nightclubbers' institution. Late-night breakfasts and lively atmosphere. *Open to 06.00.*
Lido   **4 E3**
41 Gerrard St W1. 0171-437 4431. Busy and friendly Chinese restaurant. *Open to 04.00.*
Up All Night   **6 C4**
325 Fulham Rd SW10. 0171-352 1996. Steaks, burgers and spaghetti served by lively staff. *Open to 06.00.*

LATE POST
Most post offices close at 17.30 Mon-Fri & 12.00 Sat. *However, there is one late opening office in London:*
Post Office   **4 F3**
24-28 William IV St, Trafalgar Sq WC2. 0171-930 9580. *Open 08.00-20.00 Mon-Sat.*

LOST PROPERTY
Airports
For property lost in the main airport buildings phone the British Airport Authority's Lost Property Office, Heathrow Airport, Middx. 0181-745 7727. Alternatively, contact the individual airport direct (see page 4 for a list of airports).
British Rail (trains)
If you lose something on a train, contact the station where the train you were on terminates (see page 9 for a list of London British Rail stations). They will be able to inform you whether your belongings have been recovered, and if so, where they have been taken.

London Transport (tubes) 1 B5

Lost Property Office, 200 Baker St W1 (next to Baker St Station). For enquiries about lost property please call in person (or send another person with written authority) or apply in writing (forms available at any tube station). No telephone enquiries. *Open 09.30-14.00 Mon-Fri. Closed Bank hols.*

Taxis

If you leave anything in a taxi, phone the Metropolitan Police Lost Property Office. 0171-833 0996. *Open 09.00-16.00 Mon-Fri.*

Passports

Report the loss to the police and to your embassy/high commission.

PUBLIC LAVATORIES

Look out for signs in the street directing you to the nearest public lavatory, or ask someone likely to be familiar with the area; police, traffic wardens, news-vendors and shop-keepers. All public lavatories are divided into separate areas for men and women except the newer cabin-style ones which are found in the street. These are completely self-contained and therefore unisex. They are *open 24 hrs* and you will need exactly the right coins to use them. Nearly all large department stores, museums and national art galleries have lavatories, as do pubs, mainline British Rail stations and several of the central London parks. NB: There are no public lavatories on Underground trains, nor in most Underground stations.

WHEELCLAMPING AND IMPOUNDMENT

If you are illegally parked or your vehicle is causing an obstruction, it may be wheel-clamped or towed to a pound. In either case you will have to pay a substantial fine to recover your car. If you get wheel-clamped, follow the instructions on the label attached to your vehicle. If the label is missing, phone 0171-747 4747 (24 hrs) to find out which authority to contact. This line is operated by TRACE (Tow Away, Removal & Clamping Enquiries), 1st Floor, New Zealand House, 80 Haymarket SW1 (4 E4). Open 08.00-20.00 Mon-Fri. If your car is missing, phone TRACE on the above number to find out if it has been removed to a pound and which one, how to get there by public transport and how to pay the fine.

TRACE publish visitors' guides (in English, French, German, Spanish, Italian and Dutch) giving advice on parking in London and how to avoid parking penalties. These are obtainable direct from TRACE, or from the London Tourist Board or Town Halls.

NICHOLSON

KEY TO
MAP PAGES

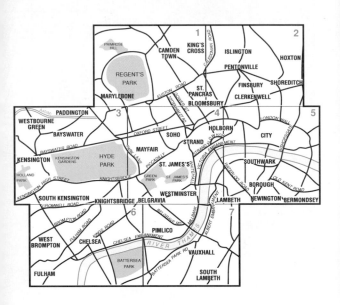

NICHOLSON
COMPUTER
MAPPING

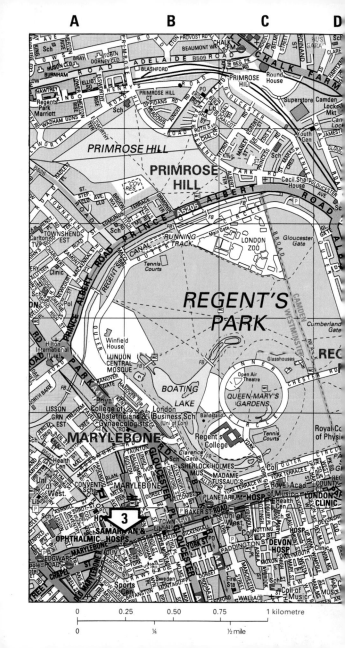

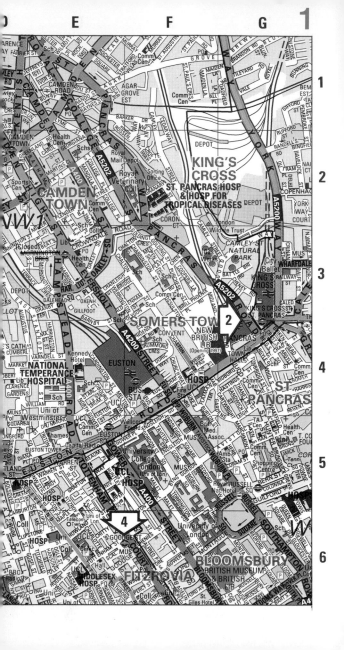

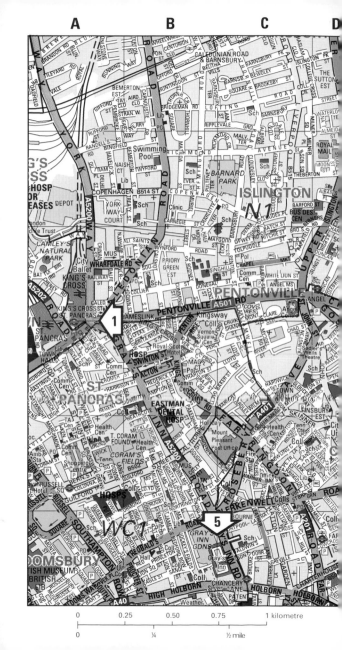

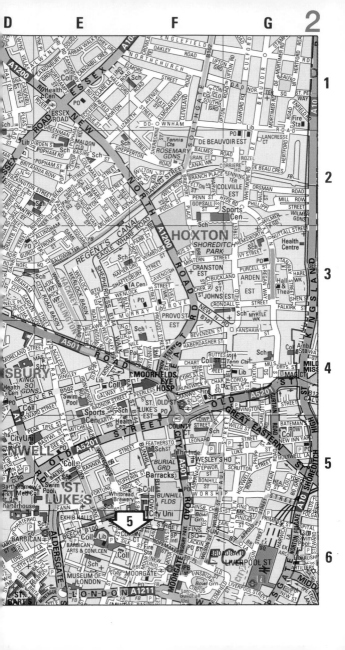

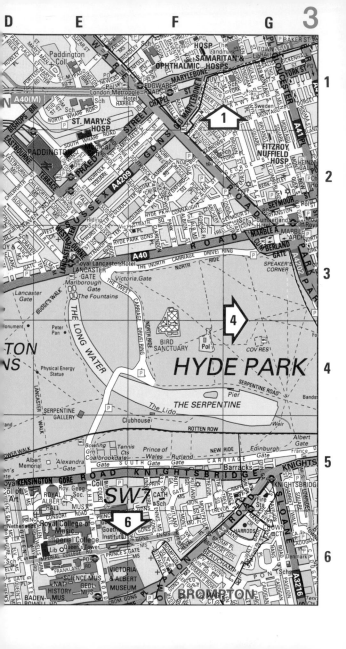

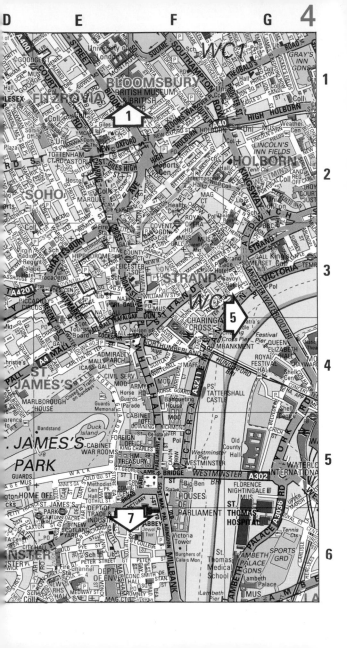

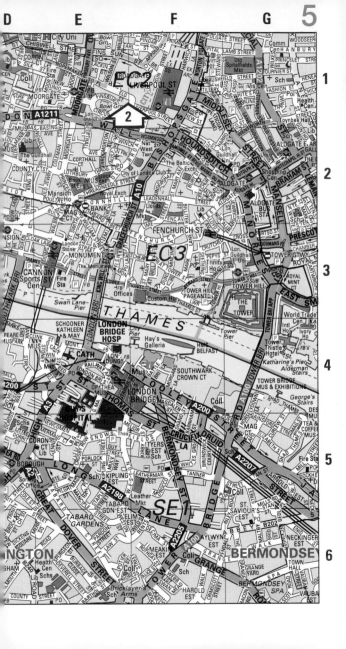

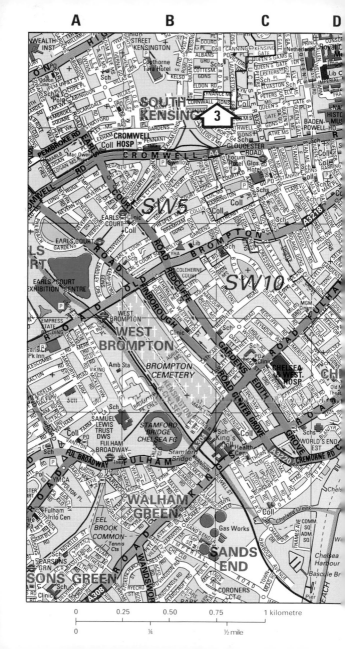

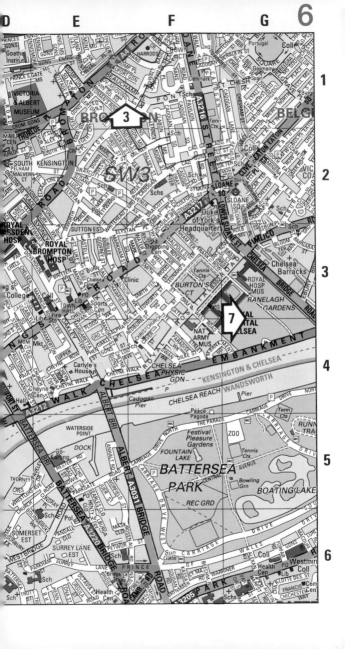

SHOPS

Aquascutum 0171 734 6090
Army & Navy 0171 834 1234
Asprey 0171 493 6767
Austin Reed 0171 734 6789
Barkers 0171 937 5432
BHS (Kensington High Street) 0171 937 0919
BHS (Oxford St) 0171 629 2011
C & A 0171 629 7272
Cartier 0171 493 6962
Christie's 0171 839 9060
Conran Shop 0171 589 7401
Covent Garden Market 0171 836 9137
DH Evans 0171 629 8800
Debenhams 0171 580 3000
Dickins & Jones 0171 734 7070
Dillons 0171 636 1577
Fenwick 0171 629 9161
Fortnum & Mason 0171 734 8040
Foyles 0171 437 5660
General Trading Company 0171 730 0411
Habitat (King's Rd) 0171 351 1211
Habitat (Tottenham Court Rd) 0171 631 3880
Hamleys 0171 734 3161
Harrods 0171 730 1234
Harvey Nichols 0171 235 5000
Hatchards 0171 439 9921
Heal's 0171 636 1666
HMV 0171 629 1240
Jaeger 0171 437 7722
John Lewis 0171 629 7711
Laura Ashley (Regent St) 0171 355 1363
Liberty 0171 734 1234
Lillywhites 0171 930 3181
Littlewoods 0171 629 7847
London Pavilion 0171 437 1838
Marks & Spencer (Ken. High St) 0171 938 3711
Marks & Spencer (Marble Arch) 0171 935 7954
Marks & Spencer (Oxford St) 0171 437 7722
Mothercare 0171 580 1688
Next (Kensington High St) 0171 938 4211
Next (Regent St) 0171 434 2515
Peter Jones 0171 730 3434
Plaza on Oxford St 0171 637 8811
Selfridges 0171 629 1234
Simpson 0171 734 2002
Sotheby's 0171 493 8080
Top Shop & Top Man 0171 636 7700
Tower Records 0171 439 2500
Trocadero 0171 439 1791
Victoria Place Shopping Centre 0171 931 8811
Virgin Megastore 0171 580 5822
Whiteley Shopping Centre 0171 229 8844

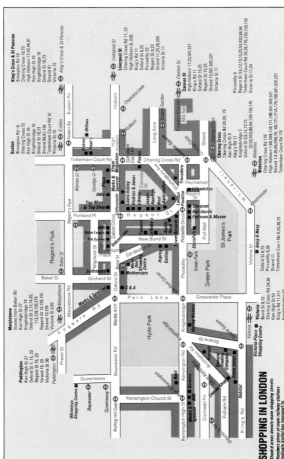

SHOPPING IN LONDON

Shaded areas denote main shopping streets
Numbers given at main railway stations
indicate useful bus transport for
shopping areas

THEATRES

Adelphi 0171 344 0055
Albery 0171 369 1730
Aldwych 0171 416 6003
Ambassadors 0171 836 1171
Apollo 0171 494 5070
Apollo Victoria 0171 416 6070
Arts 0171 836 2132
Bloomsbury 0171 388 8822
Cambridge 0171 494 5054
Comedy 0171 369 1731
Criterion 0171 369 1747
Donmar Warehouse 0171 580 8845
Drury Lane, Theatre Royal 0171 867 1150
Duchess 0171 494 5075
Duke of York's 0171 836 5122
Fortune 0171 836 2238
Garrick 0171 494 5085
Gielgud 0171 494 5065
Her Majesty's 0171 494 5400
London Coliseum 0171 632 8300
London Palladium 0171 494 5020
Lyric 0171 494 5045
Mermaid 0171 236 2211
New London 0171 405 0072
Old Vic 0171 928 7616
Palace 0171 434 0909

Phoenix 0171 369 1733
Piccadilly 0171 369 1734
Players 0171 839 1134
Playhouse 0171 839 4401
Prince Edward 0171 734 8951
Prince of Wales 0171 839 5987
Queen's 0171 494 5041
Royal Court 0171 730 1745
Royal Festival Hall 0171 928 8800
Royal National 0171 928 2252
Royal Opera House 0171 304 4000
Royalty 0171 494 5090
St Martin's 0171 836 1443
Savoy 0171 836 8888
Shaftesbury 0171 379 5399
Strand 0171 930 8800
Theatre Royal, Drury Lane 0171 494 5062
Theatre Royal, Haymarket 0171 930 8800
Vaudeville 0171 836 9987
Victoria Palace 0171 834 1317
Whitehall 0171 369 1735
Wigmore Hall 0171 935 2141
Wyndham's 0171 369 1736
Young Vic 0171 928 6363

CINEMAS

Curzon Mayfair 0171 369 1720
Curzon Phoenix 0171 369 1721
Curzon West End 0171 369 1722
Empire 0171 437 1234
Lumiere 0171 836 0691
Metro 0171 437 0757
MGM Haymarket 0171 839 1527
MGM Panton St 0171 930 0631
MGM Piccadilly 0171 437 3561
MGM Shaftesbury Avenue 0171 836 6279
MGM Swiss Centre 0171 439 4470
MGM Tottenham Court Rd 0171 636 6148
MGM Trocadero 0171 434 0031

Minema 0171 369 1723
National Film Theatre 0171 928 3232
Odeon Haymarket 0426 915353
Odeon Leicester Sq 0426 915683
Odeon Marble Arch 0426 914501
Odeon Mezzanine (Odeon Leicester Sq) 0426 915683
Odeon West End 0426 915574
Plaza 0171 437 1234
Prince Charles 0171 437 8181
Renoir 0171 837 8402
Warner West End 0171 437 4347

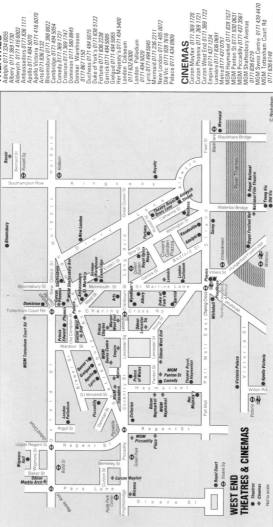

WEST END
THEATRES & CINEMAS

● Theatres
● Cinemas

Not to scale

© Nicholson

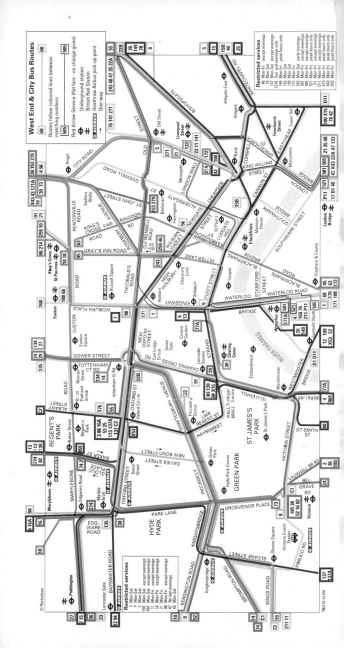

West End & City Bus Routes